INVESTIGATING

GCSE MEDIA STUDIES

Barbara Connell
Jude Brigley
Mike Edwards

Hodder & Stoughton

Orders: please contact Bookpoint Ltd, 130 Milton Park, Abingdon, Oxon OX14 4SB. Telephone: (44) 012
827720, Fax: (44) 01235 400454. Lines are open from 9.00 – 6.00, Monday to Saturday, with a 24
message answering service. Email address: orders@bookpoint.co.uk

British Library Cataloguing in Publication Data
A catalogue record for this title is available from The British Library

ISBN 0 340 758384

First published   2000
Impression number   10 9 8 7 6 5 4 3 2
Year   2005 2004 2003 2002 2001

Typeset by Fakenham Photosetting Limited, Fakenham, Norfolk
Printed in Great Britain for Hodder & Stoughton Educational, a division of Hodder Headline Plc, 338 Eusto
Road, London NW1 3BH by J W Arrowsmith, Bristol.

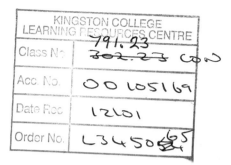
CONTENTS

Acknowledgements   v
Introduction   vi

Part 1 Exploring the Media Studies framework   **1**
1 Putting yourself in the frame   **2**
Information   2
Working definitions   2
Investigating children's picture books   4
Investigating print advertisements   6
Investigating promotional posters   13
Investigating print cartoons   17
Investigating comics   23

2 Media representations   **32**
Information   32
Part 1: Investigating the 'mags-scape'   32
Investigating typical audience signs in magazines   37
Investigating magazine front covers   41
Investigating the magazine photostory   49
Part 2: Investigating the 'docu-scape'   53

3 Media organisations: Entertainment   **67**
Inside the House of the Mouse: Team Disney   67

4 Media organisations: News and current affairs   **78**
Information   78
Why are news and current affairs productions important for media students? 78

Part 2 Studying major media industries   **91**

5 Telescapes: Popular television   **92**
Information   92
Nature and purpose of television   92
Investigating television drama 1   103
Investigating television drama 2: Genres   109
Advanced investigations: Television drama 3   113
Investigating television chat shows   116

6 Filmscapes: Reading and selling film   124

Information   124
Investigating narrative   125
Investigating identification   128
Investigating time and space   132
Investigating selling films   137
Investigating stars and genre   139
Investigating posters and trailers   142
Investigating other ways of selling   144

7 Popscapes   146

Information   146
Investigating pop music on television   150
Investigating rockumentaries   151
Investigating CD album covers   153
Investigating pop videos   156
Investigating the music press   159

8 Soundscapes: Tuning in   161

Information   161

9 Gamescapes   173

Information   173
Why is it important to study computer games?   173

10 Sportscapes   189

Information   189
Investigating sport and newspaper language   195

Information for teachers   199

Teaching resources   199

Information for GCSE candidates   201

General   201
Coursework   201
The written paper   204

Index   205

ACKNOWLEDGEMENTS

We would like to thank the many people who have helped directly and indirectly with the production of this work, in particular Tom Barrance (Media Education Wales), Cathy Grove (UNIC Publications), Ivor Hicks, Roberta Harries (Welsh Joint Education Committee) and John Ashton (Chief Examiner, GCSE Media Studies).

The authors and publishers would also like to acknowledge the following for permission to use highly edited versions of:

- the work of former students on the MA in Media Education, University of Wales Institute, Cardiff, in particular Peter Davies (Glan Ely School, Cardiff), Mandy Esseen (Stanwell School, Penarth), Sara Evans (Cardiff High School), and the work of some of their students;
- the work of students and former students of Cardiff High School and St Ilan School, Caerphilly;
- transcripts of interviews with Cassian Marriner-Edwards and Helen Iles.

None of them is personally responsible for what we have done with their work.

The authors and publishers would like to acknowledge the following for permission to use copyright material in this work:

All Action, pp. 192, 197; BBC, p. 93; EMAP Metro, p. 158; Future Publishing, p. 43; Granada Television Ltd., p. 93; HTV, p. 40; Horton Stephens, p. 6; Hyperion Books, p. 70; IPC Magazines, p. 55; Mandarin, p. 25; Melody Maker/IPC Syndication, p. 158; Poorhouse Press pp. 25, 26; Shannon Wheeler, pp. 19, 20, 21; SNK Corp. of America, p. 178; *The Guardian*, p. 59; *The Mirror*, p. 119; *The Observer*, p. 75; *The Planet on Sunday*, p. 82; The Ronald Grant Archive, pp. 72, 73, 74, 76 © Walt Disney Co., p. 137 © Lucasfilm Ltd.; The S4C Media Pack, pp. 130, 131; The Voice of the Mirror, p. 120; *The Western Mail*, p. 80; Warner Bros., p. 26.

Every effort has been made to trace copyright holders but this has not always been possible in all cases; any omissions brought to our attention will be corrected in future printings.

INTRODUCTION

Information for teachers

This book has been designed to give your students specialising in Media Studies a series of challenging investigations. We use the term 'investigation' in a variety of ways: it involves research, practical, production and presentational skills. These investigations will encourage your students to develop their media knowledge, understanding and skills in a variety of media contexts. It is our view that critical competence in Media Studies is best developed through practical/production work and its interaction with textual production and textual analysis. Students become both 'makers' and 'takers' of media texts. We aim to show how the critical dimension is created by what we term 'evaluative activity': this is the process by which your students are able to add to their understanding of the media by reflecting critically on their work at every stage of its development. The best media students have a critical 'edge'. They develop this by engaging in a wide variety of media activities both inside and outside the classroom. They are then able to apply the results of that media experience and thinking in their coursework assignments and in the written examination.

Many of your students are already independent media producers as a result of developments in technology in the last decade. It is now perfectly possible for them to produce their own web pages, to mix their own music, to produce their own fanzines and to have access to sophisticated training and a potential world audience through the World Wide Web. Recent technology has also offered the possibility for students to produce a short film with a digital video camera and carry out image editing, all with an equipment cost of about £2,000. With such software and equipment it is perfectly feasible that the shooting and editing of a short film could be accomplished in the space of a double period. However, we are also aware that 80 per cent of our fellow human beings do not even have access to a phone. Access to knowledge is a wonderful thing and is vital for development. Yet technology is like muck: no good unless it be spread. This is an issue for all of us and one that needs to be addressed in our classrooms. We hope to offer many low-tech activities (what one colleague calls 'lick and stick' activities) as well as to suggest a range of activities appropriate to the new 'mediascapes' which have emerged at the end of the twentieth century. Above all, we hope to use these activities to pose a whole range of complex and fascinating questions about our brave new world.

All the examination boards who offer GCSE Media Studies syllabuses have a structure of coursework and written examinations. The approach of each board is slightly different (as you would expect in a competition-driven examination environment). Each creates its own 'brand' of Media Studies. It is very important that you work with your examination board. This will help you to understand the nuances of interpretation that are given to terms like 'practical', 'production' and 'evaluation' in coursework and the different approaches developed for the written paper. The assignments offered in this book can be applied to all three available examination syllabuses, though you will need to tailor the work to the exact requirements of the syllabus specification with which you work to ensure the best outcomes for your students.

Our approach is based on the following principles:

● a clear conceptual framework, reflected in all of the tasks set and resources provided;

● a balance between analytic, research and creative work;

● an approach which emphasises personal response to the media, with plenty of opportunities to explore different viewpoints;

● a sensitive concern for the pleasures afforded by the media and an awareness that often the students will be more knowledgeable than the teachers in some areas.

The dynamic framework of Media Studies

Your students will develop greater understanding of and competence in exploring this framework through the knowledge and skills built up through the task-based activities in the investigations which make up this book.

Defining the terms used in the text

Media languages and texts

> 'Each medium has its own system of conveying meaning . . .'.
> *Making Movies Matter*, FEWG, 1999

The metaphors of 'language' and 'text' have been used to describe these systems. Students need, therefore, to 'write' and 'read' a variety of media in order to become 'media literate'. They need a knowledge and understanding of the 'codes and conventions' of these representational systems.

Producers and audiences

> '. . . it is an increasingly important element of basic citizenship for people to identify where messages are coming from and what motivates them'. . . Audiences are targeted and courted in many different ways, although their real interests and responses can be very hard to identify. Everyone should be able to make informed choices about their consumption . . .'.
>
> *Making Movies Matter,* FEWG, 1999

This basic relationship drives developments in the media and is an essential element of Media Studies courses. Knowledge and understanding of this relationship is a crucial element of the students' experience of making and taking media texts. Without this experience they cannot be regarded as being 'media literate'.

Messages and values

There are many theories about the media's power to affect behaviour. One key issue at stake is the media's potential effects on a range of audiences and their ideas, attitudes and beliefs. Another, and related, issue is the degree of 'representational realism' in different kinds of media texts and how they 'mediate' their relationship with the audience. These are complex issues which at GCSE level must be explored in a range of different contexts. The essential theme of this exploration is the need to distinguish between literal meanings and underlying themes. Students will explore and argue for alternative ways of representing a group, event or idea using the appropriate media language in their own work. To do so, they will need knowledge and understanding of the typical ways in which the media represent such groups, events or ideas.

Information for new Media Studies students

Welcome to a subject which has grown enormously during the 1990s. Why were you attracted to it?

Is it because:

a It is up-to-date and modern?
b It is challenging and rigorous?
c It is practical and intellectual?
d It will give you a solid grounding in the knowledge, understanding and skills required in the new millennium?

Or is it because:

a   You get to watch television, films and videos and listen to the radio in lessons?
b   You get access to the computers?
c   You learn to use a video camera?
d   You make up comics, magazines and newspapers?

Or is it that:

a   You have alternative beliefs and attitudes that you would like to promote?
b   You have a personal agenda of things you want to find out about?
c   Some areas of the media fascinate you?
d   Some areas of the media make you angry?

Or because:

a   Your friend said it was good?
b   You did not fancy anything else in the options?

A question of opinion

Activity   **Make a list of opinions you have heard recently about the following.**

Category	Opinion
1. A soap opera character	
2. A pop performer or record	
3. A world event	
4. A new computer game	
5. A football player	
6. A video or film	

Table Intro.1

Activity   Identify the different places you heard them.

Gossip with friends	
In a magazine	
On television	
Over the Internet	
On the radio	

Table Intro.2

In our view, Media Studies offers you a framework in which to develop your knowledge of the media, to understand the opinions of other people and to engage in the arguments about a central feature of all of our lives. Most of our information about the world comes from the media and they are a central feature of the way in which we entertain ourselves. Crucially, Media Studies will develop in you (depending on your attitudes and beliefs) the opportunity to find out about different media and explore through practical and production work the different ways in which they make meanings available to a variety of audiences (which will sometimes include you).

Preparatory tasks

Activity   What attitudes and beliefs can be detected in this student's approach to Media Studies?

Figure Intro. 1 What attittudes and beliefs can you detect here?

One of the things that might come out of your answers is that the student seems to equate Media Studies with watching and responding to the medium of television. Alternatively, you might feel that he has other things on his mind!

In 1997 in a GCSE Media Studies paper one of the questions referred to the terms 'media' and 'medium'. Candidates seemed to have some difficulty in identifying what these terms meant. We think it is worthwhile for you to reflect on them in order to give a sense of what we think is involved.

Working definition

A medium is a 'channel of communication' between a producer and an audience. There are many channels of communication which are together referred to as 'media'.

Activity   Study the list in Figure Intro. 2. For each category in the list:

1. Put a tick if you think it is a medium.
2. Put a question mark if you not sure.
3. Now test each category in turn by adding additional information as we have done in Table Intro. 3 for the category of films.

Films	SF novels	Computer software
Television	The Internet	Surveillance cameras
Comics	Pop music	Webcams
Newspapers	Radio	Digital sound systems
Advertisements	Cartoons	DVD
Computer games	Magazines	Videos

Figure Intro. 2

FILMS	
Type of technology involved	Film cameras, sound equipment, lights
Numbers of people reached	Mass audiences all over the world
Different channels of communication used (speaking, audio, visual)	Speaking (dialogue), sound effects, music, visual representation
Numbers of people involved in production	Large numbers of people in most countries in the world
Number of commercial or institutional owners	Many large companies (mostly American) but lots of independent producers as well
Controls and regulations	All countries have different patterns of regulation and control. In Britain we have the British Board of Film Classification.

Table Intro.3

The media are evolving at a very rapid rate under the impetus of technological development. In the modern media environment there is evidence of huge overlapping in the ways in which audiences are created by different media.

Tips

- In how many different media can you watch films?
- How many different ways can you listen to music?

Media products are affected by the ways in which they are produced and by whom they are produced.

Tips

- List your class's favourite films and television shows. Were they the same types of film or show?
- Try to identify which organisation produced them, for example Disney, Sky, BBC, Warner Brothers, ITV, MTV. In what ways are these organisations different to each other?

Media Studies is concerned with the ways and means of the modern media. It poses questions which you can investigate and find answers to.

YOU WILL NEED TO STUDY

1. how large institutions like the BBC and companies like ITV, industries like the newspaper, film and music industries, and smaller media organisations like independent animation companies produce media texts
2. how you can be a producer of media texts
3. why they and you produce media texts
4. the audience for whom they and you create media texts
5. the ways in which they and you are controlled and regulated and whether they and you should be regulated.

PART 1
EXPLORING THE MEDIA STUDIES FRAMEWORK

1 PUTTING YOURSELF IN THE FRAME

Information

- Visual images are an important part of our culture.
- They can be moving, as in film and television, or still, as in children's picture books, comics, posters, newspapers and magazines. Still visual images are a very useful starting point for media students because they are an important part of the media environment (some people like to call this 'the mediascape') but also because they are still they can draw attention to some of the features shared with the world of the audiovisual image.
- By studying the different ways in which the different media adapt and develop, you can learn about different media languages.
- The investigations in this chapter ask you to explore the important media concepts of frame, *mise-en-scène*, montage and preferred meaning and introduce you to a set of key media words to use in your investigations.

Working definitions

Add your own notes to these as you investigate the different media forms.

Frame

> 'All images have frames – the frame is the
> boundary between the image and what
> surrounds it; it is the image's edge.'
> Nick Lacey, *Image and Representation. Key Concepts in Media Studies*

Frames have different kinds of shape but most are conventional. When they are unconventional then they are significant. Frame breaking is a significant feature of many comics.

Mise-en-scène

Originally a term derived from the theatre, implying 'staging':

- it connotes setting, characters, costume and lighting;
- it concerns the movement inside the frame.

This term is important in the analysis of a wide variety of visually based media forms, especially in advertising (print- and film-based), fashion photography, magazine front covers, situation comedy, television drama, documentary, quiz or game shows and news (it is possible to use it in radio when a scene is being described in words which 'paint pictures'. Radio football commentators and news reporters are really good at this).

It can also be useful in terms of discussing sport on television. Old Trafford, the home of Manchester United, is commonly talked of as 'the theatre of dreams', for instance. In such a view, the aerial shots of the stadium and the crowd shots form part of the *mise-en-scène*. Think about the common phenomenon of 'face painting' on sporting occasions as part of *mise-en-scène*.

The term has enormous importance in film. It is primarily associated with the 'style' of particular film-makers.

Mise-en-scène concentrates on:

- setting, props, codes of non-verbal communication, dress codes, movement in the frame (panning, zooming, shot, reverse shot, etc. in film and television), eye movements in print-based environments;
- technical codes of composition: shot size, camera angle, lens type, focus, lighting codes, colour and film stock codes.

Montage

> 'Montage is the process of creating meaning through the **juxtaposition** [our emphasis] of individual shots.'
> Stuart Price, *The Complete A–Z Media & Communication Handbook*

This term is enormously important in film where the relationship of *mise-en-scène* and montage is central to a film's construction. It is also important in the production of advertisements, magazines and Web-based materials. In DTP it is important, although you may come across it more in relation to 'layering an image'. It is a central skill in certain types of animation.

Offered or preferred meaning

Images are often altered to give a particular impression. This can mean that photographs are cropped to take out any unnecessary detail that may change the meaning which is offered to the reader. For example, if you wanted to promote a sunny holiday in Spain you would not include pictures of cloudy skies, rain, crowded swimming pools and beaches heaving with people. This picture would not encourage the audience to take that holiday. However, if you wanted to take pictures which would be evidence for a travel company that it had not accurately described the hotel you stayed at you might choose images of building, workmen, rowdy holidaymakers at 3 a.m., and so on. So much depends on the reasons why you take photographs and for what kind of audience.

What is true of holiday photographs is also true for video records of real events and people.

Newspapers frequently **crop** photographs to support the stories they have written. If they want to expose an affair between a teenager and an M.P. they would want to focus totally on the couple, preferably in a compromising position. They wouldn't want to include anything that could make the relationship look innocent.

There has been a lot of discussion in the media about the ways in which modern technology can manipulate an image – to change the position of the participants, for example. If you have access to image editing software you can cause a lot of mischief with the ability of this software to change the meanings of images. Imagine putting a friend into a difficult situation by changing an image.

Image manipulation can be a bad **or** a good thing, depending on how audiences choose to interpret the image.

Captions also make a lot of difference to the way we read a picture. They help to **anchor** the meaning and are used very successfully in the print media. Captions attempt to close off particular interpretations of images so that they are read in a particular way. Of course, they do not always do this and in your discussions you should concentrate on where others agree with your interpretation and where their interpretations are different to yours. Most people tend to agree with each other so it's always interesting to think about **why** other people take a different view. It's very easy to dismiss other kinds of interpretations.

Investigating children's picture books

Activity   **Learning to read.**

Extra information
We learn from a very early age how to 'read the visual pictures' – generally long before we have learned to 'read' the words in the text.

Take a look at this picture from a child's story book and answer the questions below:

Figure 1.1   Amazing Grace

- What do you think is the story behind this picture?
- Why have you reached these conclusions?
- What types of people do you think the characters are?
- What elements of the picture have helped you to draw your conclusions?

In this simple exercise you have been demonstrating some complex skills:

- **analysing** the **denotation** of the image by identifying the main elements within it;
- **identifying** the **connotations** of the image by recognising what meanings the main elements actually convey to audiences;
- **discussing** notions of character **representation** by identifying and recognising people's character traits through elements of their physical appearance and body language.

Investigating print advertisements

 Being persuaded as a consumer.

Study the advert below:

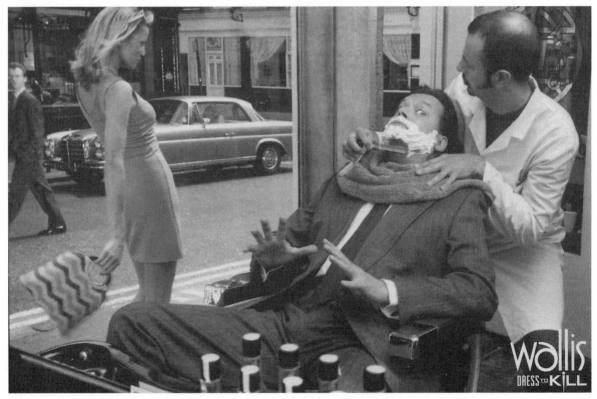

Figure 1.2   Dress to kill

Deconstruction

The image tells quite a detailed story. In order to understand it fully, you need to look at all of the separate elements that make up the picture.

Five useful tips

1. Look through the window into the street. Where do you think this scene is **set** or **located**? Obviously, it is in a city – but which one? Paris, London or New York? What evidence can you use to back up your ideas?
2. What can you tell about the **characters**? The man sitting in the barber's chair is almost certainly a wealthy businessman – we can tell this by the style of his suit and the expensive (glittering, perhaps gold?) cuff-links he is wearing. But the woman? Is she controlling the reactions of the men around her or is she oblivious to them? How would each different attitude you detect affect the way we read the picture?
3. List the denotation and connotations of the different elements which make up the image. For example:

    Denotation: Gold cuff-links   **Connotation:** Wealth/success

    Denotation: Barber's white coat   **Connotation:** Professionalism

4. Consider the position of the camera. How are we, as the audience, invited to look at this image? In media language: what is our **point of view** (PoV)? Would it make a difference to our reading of the story if we had been positioned (by the camera) on the other side of the road? Or walking towards the woman? The obvious answer is 'yes' because we would be viewing the scene from a different perspective and would miss the joke included in the image. So the point of view is important to our reading of the visual.
5. Look at the picture again. The caption 'DRESS TO KILL' contributes to the overall meaning by providing the audience with a humorous **anchor**. It relates both to the **idea** of the story (the man is literally in danger of being killed) and to the image Wallis is trying to provide for its clothes. The offered meaning is that women who wear them will be noticed and will metaphorically 'knock out' people (men) who see them. Words are important to the overall meaning of images: they work to create additional (and complementary) meanings.

Extra task
By adding some different text, either through speech bubbles or through a commentary, can you alter the picture's meanings and turn it from an advertisement into a news story, and then into a poster advertising a new Hollywood film? You can draw, trace or photocopy different elements of the original to help you with this.

It should be obvious to you now that this **story** could be **told** in a variety of ways (depending on the media form chosen and the purpose) and could be 'read' in a number of ways (for example: girls could respond in a different way to boys). You have used the same story with the same characters but in a different way. **Narrative** is concerned with the ways in which the same story can be **constructed** in different ways to give different interpretations.

Activity   Analysis of an advertisement.

Tips
Practise these key words in your work:
● denotation;
● connotation;
● representation;
● narrative;
● point of view;
● anchorage.

Select and analyse an advert of your choice. Extra marks will be credited to you for your correct usage of the key words.

Extra tips
Always consider the following when trying to work out why pictures have a certain meaning:

● **camera angles and point of view**: Does the camera tell us anything about the subject? Does it show the subject as dominant by photographing from below? Does it concentrate on particular parts of the body?;

● **lighting**: Does the light, or lack of it, create an atmosphere, perhaps of mystery or excitement? Does it come from above, below, from the side, at an angle?;

- **props**: What can you see that could tell us something about the people or the narrative?;
- **clothes**: What are the subjects wearing and what do they tell us about their hobbies, interests, occupation, age or financial situation?;
- **body language**: Do the people look relaxed, tense, excited or in control? What can you tell about them, just from the way they are posed?;
- **setting** or **location**: Does this give us any idea of where or when this photo was taken?;
- **cropping**: Has the photo been cropped in any way? If so, have you any idea what might have been left out and why?

By now you will have discovered that there are a whole range of decisions to make if you are going to construct a visual image to get the preferred meaning:

- the selection of the character types and the way they are represented;
- the point of view that needs to be clearly established;
- the background components that help to give additional meaning;
- the text which helps to reinforce our understanding of the visual.

You will probably also have worked out:

- the physical construction of the image (its denotive elements) is as important to the overall meaning as the connotative elements are;
- for example, there is no point in taking a picture of a handsome man to help sell an aftershave if pose, body language, lighting, angles, clothes, setting, locations and even background colours are not all taken into consideration.

Activity

Planning the *mise-en-scène*.

Scenario
Your brief is to design the set for a new television situation comedy based in a hotel. Design the set for the reception area, paying particular attention to the *mise-en-scène*.

Tip
Use this list of elements of the *mise-en-scène* to help you:

- background;
- props;

- informal/relaxed setting or formal/serious setting;
- lighting;
- camera angles (assume that you have three cameras);
- clothes of those who work in the space;
- furniture.

Activity

Representations of ourselves and others: constructing visual biographies and autobiographies.

Information

- This kind of activity often figures in web pages which often seek to tell the world about you, your family and your interests. It says a lot about who you are.
- The purpose of this assignment is to try to convey personal details to another member of the class who will try to read your views about yourself from the montage. (If you can put this on to a web page you can have a wider audience than a classmate and you could add voices.) If not, don't worry, it will still make a brilliant display.

Stage 1: Constructing a narrative

Rearrange some family snaps into a narrative, using the technique of **cropping**. Add **captions** to **anchor** the story.

Can you tell the story without captions?

Stage 2: Constructing a visual autobiography

Create a **montage** of pictures and words about yourself.

Tip

Study Figure 1.3.

Figure 1.3   Family snaps

Tip

To help you plan your display use these guidelines:

Planning

- Make three columns of six lines each. In the first column list six words that describe yourself, for example, 'teenager', 'fashionable', 'handsome', etc. In the second column list six things that you like and in the third column list six things that you dislike. In each case you must use only one word.
- Once you have made your list, you need to find images that represent that word – for example, if you have placed the word 'football' in your column of likes then you need to find or take a picture of a football game.
- Make a note of how you think each image represents the word that you have written down.

Design

- When you have collected all the images, design a photo-montage. You need to think of a way of displaying the pictures so that anyone who is trying to read your montage will be able to extract meanings from it. For example, how will your reader distinguish between your likes and dislikes?
- Take care when displaying your pictures. Remember that the montage itself needs to convey meaning as well as all the individual elements.
- Show your design to another member of your class whose opinion you trust. Record their responses carefully.

Evaluation

Include:

- explanations of the images chosen to represent the words you included in your original list. Be as detailed as possible in explaining the reasons for your choices. You may perhaps refer to a particular expression or an association between the image and the word. Practise using the media language you have learned;
- details of how your images were interpreted;
- your conclusions. Here you could include details of how images in general can be used to represent words or ideas; how difficult or easy it was to find images to represent your own ideas; and how well your images were interpreted by other people.

Investigating promotional posters

Audience issues

What are posters?

- Posters are 'advertising' or 'promotional' texts which occur in 'outdoor' locations, mostly roads, roundabouts and meeting places such as schools, colleges, stations, bus stops and cinemas. They are among the longest-established forms of media communication.
- They advertise and promote events, political parties, campaigns, causes, films, products and services. Where the sites are regulated they are often called 'hoardings'. Many posters are produced and placed without permission on shops which have been boarded up or on the temporary walls of building sites. This method of distributing information which trails or promotes events is often called 'fly-posting'.
- In the UK posters tend to have standard sizes:
  Fronts of shops: Double Crown
  Signs on bus shelters (40-60 inch): 4 sheets.
  Roadside (10-20 feet): 48 sheets or up to 96 sheets in some cases.
- Many of them are fixed for a short space of time and then replaced. Official sites charge their customers.

Why is it important to study posters?

- They have a long media history and raise the key issues about texts, messages and values and their relationship with audiences. They are one of the familiar parts of our media landscapes.
- They are a medium which reaches a mass audience. It has been argued that they are the last great mass medium because audiences for other media are fragmenting into smaller segments.
- Many modern posters have been very controversial in recent years, especially in relation to the use of pictures of women's bodies and the messages promoted by political parties. From them we can learn a lot about what it means to live in our society.
- They are often linked to other campaigns being conducted in a wide range of media which allow different media languages to be explored from a common starting point. The ways in which they create messages can be compared in the different media.
- The technology of roadside advertising is changing as it becomes more electronic and this raises important questions about the role of technology in modern life.

- Posters offer good ways of getting your point of view across to a wide variety of people on an issue or service which concerns you.

- You can use them to protest.

Activity　　**Studying posters.**

Good media production is always based on research. You need to study where posters are sited, the kinds of audience who will be attracted, the way they look at the posters (in the car, waiting for a bus, having a coffee, going to the toilet) and how they work as media communication. You may even be surprised at just how many posters you find on your typical journeys.

Task 1: Collecting the evidence

The most popular places are obviously the places where most of the people you want to see a poster are likely to see it. List some of your typical journeys. Count the type, size and number of the posters you encounter on three typical journeys, for example:

- from home to the cinema,
- from school to the town centre,
- from your home to a relative in another town within your area.

Task 2: Identify the main elements

Use the list below to help you:

- brand/issue/service advertised;
- location;
- size;
- key words used;
- pictures on poster;
- audience appeal.

Task 3: Poster conventions

Posters have three main elements:

- a picture;
- a brand name/issue/service;
- printed text.

Posters have to attract attention to themselves by:

- making promises in words and images;
- using strong and bold colours;
- using large, bold type.

Stage 1

Choose any poster presently on display in your school or college.

- Identify the name, issue or service to which this poster draws attention.
- Describe the picture in your own words.
- Note the different colours used on each of its elements and where they are used.
- Roughly how much of the poster is taken up by pictures? How much by the type used?

Stage 2

Review any other posters you have access to.

Do they all follow the conventions? Some will and some will not. When posters do not follow the rules the reason is nearly always the same: the producers are always on the lookout for a different way of appealing to the audience so they look to bend the rules in some way.

Stage 3

See if you can find examples from your research of these ways of appealing to the audience:

- visual or verbal puns;
- puzzles or questions;
- funny, distorted (surreal) or pretty pictures;
- two different elements put side by side (juxtaposed);
- famous people or recognisable cartoon characters;
- commands.

Stage 4

Study the film posters in Figure 1.4. Use the information to explain how they appeal.

Figure 1.4.

Task 4:   Poster locations

Here are some criteria for 'good' sites for posters:

- places where most of the people you are aiming the poster at congregate or pass;
- places where it is easy to see the poster;
- places which allow people's attention to be drawn to the poster;
- places which will not offend people;
- places which are big enough for the poster.

Stage 1

Using a map of your immediate area, put flags in for each poster your class finds.

Stage 2

Colour-code in terms of type of poster, size of poster and products advertised or promoted.

Stage 3

Analyse your findings visually in a chart or diagram for display in your classroom.

Stage 4

Find out the name of each firm who is responsible for siting the poster. Look up their costs on the Internet. For example, you will find Maiden, who own a lot of roadside sites, at www. maiden.co.uk.

Investigating print cartoons

'Let Me Entertain You'

What are cartoons?

They can best be described as humorous illustrations or strips of illustrations which tell a story or comment on the human condition.

> 'Cartoons may be called the slang of graphic art. Like verbal slang, they tend to rely for their impact on spontaneity, playfulness, popular imagery and often deliberate vulgarity . . .'.
> J. Geipel (1972)

Why is it important to study them?

- They have an even longer media history than the promotional poster and can be studied in their own right.
- In the present media environment, they are an important element of newspapers. Every major newspaper has cartoonists who seek to comment on a whole range of news from a variety of different viewpoints. Many of these are famous in their own right for providing insightful commentary on the strange, absurd, funny and wonderful things human beings get up to.
- You will also find this kind of visual humour in some types of birthday cards which often tend to exploit the bizarre and surreal elements of life.

How do they work?

Activity   **Having a laugh.**

Remember that often in examples you will find different elements of the categories listed below.

Stage 1
Study the cartoons in Figures 1.5 and 1.6 and any other examples you have.

Stage 2
Find examples of the different kinds of humour.

Stage 3
Categorise your findings using the information below.

Humour categories

1. **Recognition humour**
   For any illustration to work as humour, the audience has to recognise that what is depicted is a part of human experience. People and their ways are at the basis of the experience of the cartoon.
2. **Humour with a message**
   The aim of this is both to entertain and to inform you by exposing the absurdity and senselessness of something. This can be a personal and social thing.

Figure 1.5 Source: Shannon Wheeler

Figure 1.6   Source: Shannon Wheeler

3. **Visual puns**

   These work by playing off the qualities associated with one visual object against another visual object. The outcome can be an amusing, surreal, grotesque, bizarre or shocking comment.

4. **Wacky or zany**

   The world is turned upside down and inside out.

5. **Bitter humour**

   In this humour there is real anger. It seeks to expose the ridiculousness, self-righteousness and pomposity of human beings. It is humour with a snarl.

Activity   **Telling a story: The single frame narrative.**

Study Figure 1.7.

Figure 1.7   Source: Shannon Wheeler

Stage 1

Narratives told by the media do the hard work of connecting and organising events and thoughts for us. **What connects this story together?**

Stage 2

You are involved in this media narrative because you help it to mean something by making your own interpretations, based on previous knowledge and experience as well as information given in the text. This would not work unless there was a boy and a girl and a sense of what should normally happen when they go to the pictures or shopping together in most Western societies. Dating is a situation full of difficulties. **Where is this story set?**

Stage 3

Other cultures will have a very different sense of 'going to the pictures' and of 'boys and girls' being unaccompanied. This 'normal' activity of 'dating' could be very shocking. The plots of 'Bollywood' films are interesting from such a point of view. **Discuss the idea of 'dating' and its pleasures and pitfalls.**

Activity   **Revising deconstruction.**

- To reveal the structure of this single frame, it becomes necessary to analyse or to deconstruct it.
- To deconstruct a text is to attempt to undo, or see behind, the work of media producers.
- Plot and story. There is a difference between the story and the plot, even in this single frame narrative.

Tell the story. Very easy for most of you, we guess.

Now explain how the story was told. Was this more difficult?

Revising plot

- This gives the audience one piece of information in a speech bubble which is matched by the second speech bubble.
- The convention in the West is to read visually from left to right and that helps us to understand the frame. The audience (you) becomes involved in making sense of the events and information in the order in which they are given in the speech bubbles.
- This method of organising events is known as 'plotting'.

Would this narrative work if you read the second speech bubble first?

Revising the narrator and point of view

- The role of who is telling the story, that is, from whose viewpoint the audience is told the tale, is crucial to the study of narrative.
- It is the job of the narrator to tell the story to the audience. In this case the narrator is outside the story, constructing it, and knows both sides.

Revising the *mise-en-scène*

- A clear emphasis on character through the eyes and lips especially (body language).
- Setting is lightly sketched in.

Investigating comics

> 'It's only lines on paper, folks!'
> R. Crumb, 1969

Information

- What comic producers have to do is to encompass all human actions and emotions in **narratives** which amuse, divert, entertain or inform. They only have lines to represent all of this. They have to represent speech, actions and behaviour, thoughts, senses, ideas, emotions and expressions, and they do it by drawing lines.
- In many ways it is obvious that we 'read' comics in that we sit and turn the pages just like a book. However, when we read comics we do not simply read the words. The comic reader is required to exercise both visual and verbal interpretative skills to make sense of the comic. While comics are clearly different from films (they do not move and do not have sound), they do have much in common with them.
- There is also a strong cross-over from comic book characters to film heroes and heroines like Batman, Superman and Judge Dredd. Xena: Warrior Princess went from TV character to comic book character in a reversal of this process. The cross-over is even more marked when we think about the animated 'stars' of computer games like the Super Mario Brothers or Lara Croft or Sonic the Hedgehog.

Working definitions

- A **panel** is the equivalent of a page in a book.
- It is made up of **frames** which link together to tell the part of the story on the page. Some panels are a single frame.
- Framing is an important element because the frames **link** the action together and allow the audience to follow the story.
- A **shot** is the way in which the comic illustrator chooses the **point of view** from which to view the action in the frame.

Activity   **Investigating typical conventions.**

Extra information

Comic artists are constantly striving to make the medium serve their purposes and are always looking for creative ways of using the typical codes and conventions. The best way of researching these is to study a range of comics.

Study the following examples as your starting point for further research.

Linear representation of motion/speed, energy and effort
See Figure 1.8.

Linear representation of speech and sound (snoring, whistling and clapping)
See Figure 1.9.

Linear representation of smell, thought, emotion and mood
See Figure 1.10.

Framing strategies

- The comic works by sequencing segments of the story into panels or frames.
- The movement between the frames or panels must be logical to the reader. The openness of the single frame with its tendency to **open** interpretation has to be **closed off** by the next frame or panel, which also remains open for the closure of the next frame. In this way there is a logic in the order of the frames or panels.
- This implies a contract or pact between the author or artist and you, the reader. You both seek to understand each other's intentions.

Figure 1.8   *Source:* Comics and Sequential Art, Will Eisner, Poorhouse Press

Figure 1.9   *Source:* Comics and Sequential Art, Will Eisner, Poorhouse Press

Figure 1.10

Activity

Task 1: Narrative continuity
Plan some six-frame narratives.

Tips
Invent a character based on a part of the body. Use Figures 1.11 and 1.12 as visual tips.

Figure 1.11   Based on the work of Sebastianiou Kocijoncic, Glan Ely School, Cardiff

Figure 1.12   Based on the work of Sebastianiou Kocijoncic, Glan Ely School, Cardiff

Activity   Is the language of comics a universal language?

Task 1
Study the examples of Japanese comic pages in Figure 1.13.

Stage 1
How much do you understand from simply looking at the visual illustration?

Stage 2
How much could you 'read'?

Stage 3
Does everyone in your group agree on the narrative (the way the story is told)?
Does every one agree on the story (what it is about)? Does it make a difference
if you read from right to left?

Stage 4
Following the discussion, try to identify the stories from the descriptions
below:

1. Yohel and his younger brother experience a little posture
   straightening while learning to meditate.
2. A lawyer defending five young men accused of raping a 14-year-old
   girl visits the girl's house. He introduces himself to the victim's
   mother.
3. Buddhist and Shinto factions in the palace jockey for influence, and
   the young prince explains why a rainmaking ceremony won't work.
4. After talking things over with her younger boyfriend, the woman
   announces to her children that he will be living with them.
5. In front of the boss, a co-worker demands to know Tanaka's true
   opinion, which the poor man doesn't have.

Task 2: Tackling stereotypes

Extra information
- The key concept you will need to work with in this section is
  'stereotyping'. From the outset it is important to grasp that we all use
  stereotypes and stereotyping to help us make sense of the world. They
  are our conventional ways of seeing people, events and things in the world.
  And just as the world changes, so do many of our ways of seeing and
  interpreting the world.
- The world of the media offers multiple ways to respond. The key issue is
  how we use these ways of looking in our day-to-day existence. We all need

29

Figure 1.13

to challenge and test our assumptions and commonsense ways of looking at the world. If necessary we may need to change our ways of looking. That's why your opinion is so important and studying the ways and means of the media can help you with what sometimes can be a painful and challenging process.

Working definitions

- Process of 'categorisation'
  This helps us make sense of the world by offering easy ways to 'read' the signs. When abroad or in a strange place, for instance, it is important to take precautions to protect yourself. You do this by studying the signs or indications of potential problems and being 'streetwise'. Signs are not always a complete proof of problems but we sometime ignore them at our peril.
- 'Short cuts'
  They allow us to identify things quickly and simply. These kinds of short cuts are very important in the media in areas like **genre recognition** and **audience identification**.
- 'Labelling' and 'exaggeration'
  Stereotypes have their basis in the world we live in and have a relationship to the power structures which tie societies together. As such they can be positive or negative. Attitudes to certain kinds of stereotypes clearly change and media productions often reflect the way in which these are changing.

Stereotypes, then, are crucially bound up in the way we represent the world to ourselves. They often feel like 'common sense'.

2 MEDIA REPRESENTATIONS

Information

- Representation is concerned with the ways in which media producers (which includes you) construct both fictional and real events and people.
- It is an inevitable and necessary process in media production.
- The name of this process is **mediation**. Between the event and its representation a process takes place which changes the event or person. In simpler terms, the process explores the relationship of the media producer and the responses of the media audience.
- The technology used makes a difference to the ways in which events and people are represented.

Why is representation important?

- As a student of the media and a media consumer, you need to look carefully at the dominant patterns of representation in our society. Most of us accept these most of the time.
- To be a critical media student means both to **question** where our opinions and images come from by deconstructing **typical** representations and to **work on** ways of reconstructing them using the ways and means of the modern media and to **produce** ideas of your own, based on the questions you ask yourself about how best to represent. them

Part 1: Investigating the 'mags-scape'
General information on magazines

- In the past 10 years the number of magazines published has risen by a third. You only have to look in your newsagent's or supermarket or local store to see evidence of this. There are a huge number of **titles** which are organised on the shelves in very specific ways at the **point of sale.**
- Magazine publishers are able to cater to small-scale tastes and interests: they have pioneered the **systematic targeting of particular audiences**. Mainstream television has so far not been able to compete with specialised magazines because

they are able to reach minority audiences that other media have to neglect. The growth of Internet-based 'magazines' might yet challenge this assumption.

- Women's magazines continue to be strong sellers and there has been a recent growth of men's non-pornographic general interest titles, such as *GQ*, *Esquire*, *Loaded* and *FHM*, associated with the fashionable concept of 'laddishness', i.e. a focus on football, drinking, 'birds' and 'man-things'.

- Magazines associated with development in technology, especially computers, have become a significant part of the market.

- The linkage to television especially, film and music has been an important development, particularly in terms of what has been called 'lifestyle' programming on television: cooking, make-over shows, antiques, gardening, hobbies, film review programmes, the wide variety of programmes about pop music and all the different mixes of these.

- The linkage of the titles of magazines to television programmes is growing as the mass audience for television begins to disintegrate under the pressure of more choice of channels. These publications are also linked to websites.

- This aspect can be related to patterns of ownership. Magazines are often published by companies who have a wide diversity of business and media interests in areas such as television, radio, newspapers and the Web, all of which though separate enterprises seek to feed off each other in order to make profits for the companies' shareholders.

Tip

It is always worth finding out more about the diversity of business interests of major media organisations. The *Guardian's The Media Guide* is an excellent starting point.

- Magazines exist by discovering and analysing social attitudes and selling their product to people attracted to them. They clearly **target** audiences and send out information in the form of media packs to attract potential advertisers. They are attractive to advertisers as they create a unique environment in which to sell their products.

- Magazines often act like an advertisement as well as carry advertisements.

- The placement of advertisements in relation to particular features of the magazine – advertisers pay higher **premiums** for more favoured spots or for spots which link to their product – is as important as it is in television advertising.

- Magazines are strongly associated with leisure and 'time to yourself'. More than any other media product, they are easy to drop in and out of. Because of the way they are read – by flicking and finding points of interest – particular attention needs to be given to the ways in which the magazine is organised to lead the reader. **Trailing** and **listing** features through a variety of means is central.

●   Attention also needs to be given to the organisation of the layout of **facing pages** from the point of view of **narrative continuity**.

Target audience: 'Attention grabbers'and 'first impressions'

Working definition

Media identification

The concept of '**media identification**' proposes a link between the '**signs**' of the production and the '**audience**' which receives them as '**cues**' or '**prompts**'. The key idea is of '**hailing**' the '**target audience**': it is a '**recognition sign**', like saying 'hello', which looks for a response from someone else. When you first encounter someone in the real world you usually want to make an impression unless you want to forget the whole encounter. A media production also has to draw attention to itself or else there is little point in producing it. It has to stand out from the crowd. The way it appeals at first sight or on first hearing is central. It is also, therefore, an '**announcement**' sign which asks you to 'listen' or 'look at me'.

Activity   **Magazine research.**

Task 1: Research

Stage 1: Collecting
Collect a range of magazines. Allocate about three magazines to a group. (To widen the investigation, exchange the magazines after a certain period of time.)

Stage 2: Analysing
Study the main elements – photographs, captions, design, features, etc.

Stage 3: Classifying
Fill in the categories in Table 2.1.

Stage 4: Presentation
Finally, discuss your findings (you will certainly have extra categories).

1 Elements of the magazine which the group thought were shocking and sensationalist	
'Wow' (as in 'amazing')	
'Wow' (as in 'cool')	
'Wow' (as in 'riveting' and 'compelling')	
'Urgh' (as in 'horrible')	
'Urgh' (as in 'stomach-churning' or 'sick-making')	
2 Elements which were funny or humorous	
Eh? (as in ambiguity of all kinds, especially puns)	
Ah! (as in 'nudge nudge, wink wink' approaches, suggestiveness)	
3 Elements to do with the relationship between the sexes	
Phwoah! (as in 'fanciable' and 'cute' or 'neat' and as found in images of desire, perfection, adulation, worship)	
4 Elements to do with confessions, secrets, gossip, bragging	
Listen! (as in 'do you want to know what?')	
5 Elements to do with emotional appeal	
Arrh! (as in 'cute', with babies, animals, children, animated figures especially)	
6 Elements to do with elite persons	
Look or listen to who is here! (as in star or celebrity endorsement)	

Table 2.1

Task 2
Take each category. Discuss examples of such appeals in the listed media forms and genres.

- Film
- Television
- Computer games
- Radio
- Posters.

Tips

- Choose still images and moments you remember from film and television, incidents or characters, etc.
- Make into lists of, for instance, the most 'gross' moments in film, 'scary' moments on television, 10 posters to make you 'puke', the world's 'worst' pop songs, best 'snogs' on television, 'cool' features of music videos.

Stereotypes again.

- They function quickly to identify a point of contact with the audience and create short cuts for the audience. We do not pick up magazines off the shelf unless we are initially attracted at the point of sale or we have heard about them from other people.
- We only continue to flick through the magazine if we find what we want in it. We buy the magazine because it meets our interests.
- As such, magazines tap into patterns of representation about maleness or girls or women or ethnicity or children or age or nationality, in fact, any aspect of the audience which the producer needs to address in order to persuade the buyer.
- You cannot have a media production which does not have an audience so you cannot have a magazine that does not use stereotypes. Media productions which you might think of as 'weird' or 'stupid' share this in common with media productions which you happily consume and accept.
- What magazines use stereotypes **for** is a very different issue and tells you an enormous amount about the target audience!

Working definition

Intertextuality
This idea suggests that all texts refer to other texts.

Almost certainly, you will have needed to refer to other kinds of media productions in your discussions and not only because we suggested it. Because the world of the media is one in which media producers compete for the audience they use a range of repeated strategies which are rarely original. They build on existing productions and try to add something of their own. All media producers have a strongly formed sense of what other media producers are doing; not only in their area of media production but in the wider world of media production.

Any discussion of representations raises complicated issues.

Be prepared for:

- people who insist that they are right and everyone else is wrong;
- people who accept one aspect or element but not another;
- people who use different examples out of their own media experience;
- some passionate opinions and excellent debate.

Investigating typical audience signs in magazines
Information

Some conventional meanings of signs

Position/point of view signs

- High: dominance/authority
- Head on: challenging, rebellious
- Low: subservience, inferiority
- Side on: teasing, aversion, villainy, enigmatic

Treatment signs

Angle of lighting on image of person or location:

- Front: ageless, bland, nondescript
- Back: gives depth, emphasises pattern, creates contours
- Top: youthfulness, spirituality
- Side: unsure, indecisive, morally ambiguous
- Bottom: sinister, scary, spooky, villainous

Colour signs

- Blue: authority and the law, sea, cool, often associated with men
- Pink: sweetness, tenderness, innocence, traditional femininity

- Red: danger, sin, warmth, passion, excitement, fire
- Black: dangerous, dark, sinful, dramatic, serious, melancholic, sad, documentary, truth
- Purple: royalty, luxury, decadence
- Yellow: cheery, sun, bright, happy, mellow, heat (makes objects look bigger)
- White: hygiene, purity, doctors, nurses, hospitals, virginal innocence
- Green: earth, natural, fertility, country, fresh
- Gold: precious, rare, wealth

Colour combinations add to this, for example police and nurses with blue and white uniforms, characters dressed in black and red like Dracula.

Linguistic signs

Verbs
- Descriptive, evoking senses, frequent use of 'get'.
- Lots of action: go, make sure, book now.

Nouns
- Lots of names of things and people.
- Often compounded, like 'girl power'.

Adjectives
- Lots of them. Compounded, for example 'minty fresh'.
- 'Floating', as in 'bigger, whiter, greater, more extravagant/exciting than'.

Neologisms
- Two common words combined (for example 'fangtastic' for a new toothpaste with white and red paste).

Similes
- Often easier than metaphors.

Word order
- Simplified and edited to bare essentials: 'Be there. Be first. Be brilliant'.
- Lots of colloquialisms ('cool', 'gross') and different kinds of spellings of common words (KwikSave).

Emotive words
- Looking to create a whole range of reactions: 'You want it, we got it', excitement, incitement, etc.
- Creation of desirable attributes for the product.

Catch phrases
- For example, 'Every little helps', 'Everyone's favourite store'.

Activity   Design your own magazine advertisement.

General tips
- Choose a product: emphasise its newness, recency, innovative or improved nature.
- Choose the group you want to target.
- Build in a whole series of audience cues.

The three key elements
1. **Name of product**: give it a 'personality'; link it to a consumer need, desire or wish.
2. **The visual image**: appeal to the target audience and its lifestyle.
3. **The anchoring captions**: make claims, persuade, use emotive words, simplify.

Appeal directly:
- create a set of connotations for the product based around these three elements of the production;
- make a promise to the consumer of the product through the combination of the three elements.

Activity   Analysing an advertisement.

Task

Stage 1
Study the advertisement in Figure 2.1.

Stage 2: Answer the questions

Starter questions:
1. What product is being advertised? In what kind of media production will you find such an advert?
2. List the different visual images used to construct the advertisement.
3. How have the images been used?
4. How does the reader become involved in advertisement?
5. List two kinds of audiences the advertisement is aimed at.
6. What are the promises of this advertisement?

More advanced questions:
Study the text-marked version of the same advertisement in Figure 2.2.

Activity Media effects.

Extra information

- In the past, it was thought that media products had a direct link to opinions and actions.
- This was sometimes called the '**hypodermic**' effect. Some critics of certain kinds of media productions proposed that they were addictive and their effects could be injected like a drug.
- In recent times it has been found that audiences are not so easily influenced. Researchers have found that audiences are not simply '**passive**' consumers of media productions but take an '**active'** control over responses to them. They are not 'duped' by the media but use them in sophisticated and intelligent ways.

Working definitions

The active audience

> '. . . the idea that audiences are not misled by broadcasters and other powerful forces, but are intelligent and discriminating, capable of interpreting messages and of "negotiating" meaning.'
> Stuart Price

Uses and gratifications

> '. . . a theory of textual consumption which emphasises audiences' use of what they see, hear and read. Media texts are thought to provide information, reinforcement of identity and values, integration into the social environment, and entertainment.'
> Stuart Price

Task

Mount a defence of your favourite magazine or television soap. Use clippings and examples to help you make your case.

Tips

- How do you use it? When? In what circumstances?
- Are there features of the magazine you particularly relate to or people or situations in soaps?
- Do your share your pleasure with others? Chat? Gossip?
- Does the production help you learn anything about issues in the 'real' world?

Genre

Extra information

- The cover serves to label not only the magazine but the consumer who possesses it. The most common strategy is to create an idealised reader image. This image is rich in secondary connotations.
- Smaller photos often surround the primary icon, offering patterns of repetition and reinforcement.

Figure 2.3

Source: Future Publishing

Activity   **Images of people.**

Task 1
Use the cover image from the magazine *PC Format* in Figure 2.3.

Text-mark it.

Tips
- Costume/clothes
- Props
- Body language
- Point of view signs
- Treatment signs.

Task 2
Change the photograph in some way.

Tips
- Put a different face on the body.
- Draw a beard or moustache on the face.
- Cross-dress the image by cutting and pasting.

Extra tip
If you can change the meaning of the photographs by substitution you are in the presence of an **alternative representation**.

Extra information

Drawings
Key elements to look for in representations of the drawn body:

- Squashing, stretching, elongating, miniaturising.
- Body can be fragmented, broken, shattered.
- Body can be reassembled using different objects and materials.
- Substitutions of parts for whole (eggs for eyes, sausage for smile).
- Bodies can be represented as machines and vice versa (especially in SF), with a life of their own.
- Impossible abilities – eyes that stretch on coils; recoiling arms; extending lips; it can fly, lift impossible objects and weights, experience violence without pain.
- Express extremes of emotion: maniacal grins, slavering chops, grotesque smiles, contorted physical responses.
- Reduced or enlarged or aspects of both in same body – small head, huge hands (think Popeye or Lara Croft, if you must).
- Change gender by blurring the distinction between male and female, age

by smoothing out the effects of age or adding the effects, racial identities by changing the face or clothes (by techniques like morphing and image manipulation).

Advanced Activity — Researching gender representations.

Extra information: Gender display

- The female body is one of the most densely packed of all signs in modern society. However, the male body has also begun to arouse as much attention in recent years. Representations of the body on some front covers have changed. However, in most cases the representation of gender on front covers still remains the perfect, unattainable goal for most people.
- It is a very controversial area – anorexia, eating disorders, role models, patterns of male dominance, unattainable ideals, stereotyping of what it means to be 'attractive' in order to sell products are areas of intense concern in society.
- You can learn to analyse the typical connotations of signs which usually arise in the areas of both male and female representation and so develop your own opinions based on evidence.

Task 1

Start by collecting examples and use your examples to reinforce or challenge the categorisations in the list below. Then, using examples, present your evidence as a talk or a report. Lead the discussion on the issues raised.

- Head and body tilting – where the head is pushed forward or whether a part of the body is highlighted.
- Lowering of head, fluttering of eyelashes and looking down are conventionally interpreted in many cultures as submissive, passive and sometimes 'come on' signs.
- Representations which reveal a lack of seriousness: child-like, kittenish, playful poses, broad expansive smiles, wide open eyes. Typically, they indicate 'cuteness', innocent sexuality, trust – fur, cuddly toys, animals often part of *mise-en-scène*.
- Images of bashfulness, casual and trusting postures, knees bent, arms behind main part of body (but not on hips). Suggests openness and trust – relying on others' goodwill.
- 'Licensed withdrawal'. Do the hands cover the eyes, lips, part of face (can be a veil or a shadow)? Suggests obedience, mystery, secrets, intrigue, enigma.
- Aversion of eyes. Can suggest shame, secrets.

- Unfocused gaze – sexuality, dreaming.
- Staring eyes – especially in close-up – is a powerful experience: very common in drawn images to suggest demonic possession (think of the 'staring eyes' image of Tony Blair, or the wolves in a recent advertisement about car security).
- Eyes which meet the gaze of the viewer – contact (across a crowded room), challenge (heroes), come-on (think pin-up girls/the *Sun*/'Baywatch'/pop magazines). NB In cultures which do not understand the Western conventions of the camera this is not always the case.
- Exaggerated emotional display – smiles, tears, laughter, arms in the air. Tends in many cultures to connote 'women' who are traditionally supposed to show such open emotion.

(Based on categories described by E. Goffman.)

Activity   Yourself as a stereotype.

Task 1
Study the series of photographs called 'Little Miss . . .' in which Jessica Winston, a former student at Cardiff High School, takes photographs of herself (Figure 2.4).

Task 2
Explain how she has used:
- aspects of the concept of *mise-en-scène*;
- references to other kinds of media productions

to help her construct the series' (**intertextuality**).

Task 3
Plan your own series of photographs (with yourself as the model) which explore typical representations of teenagers.

Tips
- Research teenage magazines (and the media generally) for typical representations.
- Challenge typical representations if you want to.

Advanced Activity   Cindy Sherman.

Using the Web, find out about the American photographer Cindy Sherman. Give an illustrated talk to the group about her work.

LITTLE MISS ... ELEGANT   LITTLE MISS ... SPORTY   LITTLE MISS ... TRASHY

Little Miss Elegant is a typical teenage type. She is the would-be sophisticate who is always seen at all the right parties, probably wearing her mother's shoes. This girl wears concealer because she would like to have bags under her eyes. To her boys are an escort.

With this girl, forget the doughnuts and bring on the mineral water. No couch potatoes need apply. To Little Miss Sporty boys equal friends but she knows all the cute ones. This girl is the original fitness freak, her trainers cost more than your car.

Little Miss Trashy dresses for others instead of herself. She takes being called 'bimbo' as a compliment. She is always loud; the girl is probably drunk and, anyway, loud attracts attention. Summing up Little Miss Trashy, one would say, too few clothes and not enough brain. To her boys equal life.

Figure 2.4a   *b*   *c*

LITTLE MISS ... NERD

Little Miss Nerd is the swot who gets called teacher's pet. She is weird, i.e. loves learning for its own sake! Little Miss Nerd is an introvert who thinks boys are computer partners. To this girl work is life and she would rather lift a book than a beer.

LITTLE MISS ... AMBITIOUS

Little Miss Ambitious is power-hungry; threaten and she will bite. This girl is very sly. She is only your friend when you can do something for her. She is upwardly mobile. Her main aim in life is to achieve yuppie status. To her boys are colleagues.

LITTLE MISS ... HIPPY

Little Miss Hippy is an earth child, at ease with herself and at home in the world. She always finds time for star-gazing. Little Miss Hippy thinks trees are easily as important as people. To her boys are only good for digging protest tunnels.

Figure 2.4d

e

f

Investigating the magazine photostory

Information

What are photostories?

- An amalgamation of comic techniques (use of frames, panels and speech/thought bubbles, etc.) and photographs.
- They have a high degree of 'realism'. They tell 'true-to-life stories' representing 'real' people in 'real' places facing 'real' problems.
- Typical emotional problems and moral problems besetting the teenager/young people.
- Often an agony column or problem page acted out.
- Case histories, test cases or demonstrations.
- Connections with the family snap: domestic, family and relationship concerns and questions of class identity.
- The use of photographs emphasises their closeness to 'real' life.
- Similarly, the emphasis tends to be on the standard photo, suggesting that presentation of evidence is straight and direct.

How do they work?

- Character-led: the emphasis is always on the issues or challenges facing the characters.
- Foreground is occupied by the characters. The face and pose are central: tendency for conventional shots (mid and knee upwards: extreme close-up is rare).
- Typical and simple ways of telling stories: a problem is posed, developed (nearly always in relation to other people) and a resolution offered.
- The narrative can be 'open' (as in a series with 'cliff-hangers') or 'closed' (as in a final resolution).
- They are simple puzzles looking for a clear-cut solution.
- Captions and speech balloons reinforce and anchor the offered/preferred meaning.
- The words are like a written script which has been planned before the photographs were taken.

Why are they important?

- In many ways they are an example of a feature of magazines which are less popular than it used to be. They have figured less frequently in magazines and newspapers in the 1990s. However, like many media phenomena pronounced 'dead' they have a habit of coming to life in new ways. The Activities suggest ways in which you might be able to develop this feature.

- They have an important part to play in print-based material as exemplars and are very useful in explaining complex issues simply. The *Guardian* newspaper sometimes uses them in this way and many of your textbooks use photographs in sequences to tell stories. Some magazines still use them, as do some popular newspapers.

Activity

Planning a typical photostory involving teenagers.

Stage 1
Choose a typical situation with which you are faced in your everyday life. Romance is a typical concern.

Stage 2
Choose your actors and research locations.

Stage 3
Write the script. Include the words the actors actually speak and thoughts they have as speech/thought/dreaming bubbles and the accompanying captions.

Stage 4
Plan and rehearse the 'takes', thinking very carefully about typical framing (see Chapter 1) and making sure you construct all the elements of the story into a satisfying narrative.

Tip
Most British photostories tend to have eight or nine frames on a page.

Stage 5
Research the kinds of magazines which feature your kind of story.

Stage 6
Present your photostory to another group. Explain to them what you were trying to do and the media approaches you used. Explain how you plan to **distribute** the final production.

Tips
- You might not want to do all of these tasks in this order.
- Make sure you evaluate each stage.

Activity Using the photostory experimentally to illustrate poems and song lyrics.

Along the icy street

The first ice of human hurt. The first ice of human hurt. The first ice of human hurt. The fir
human hurt. The first ice of human hurt. The first ice of human hurt. The
of human hurt. The first ice of human hurt. The first ice of human hurt.
the first ice of human hurt. The first ice of human hurt. The first ice of hum
rt. The first ice of human hurt. The first ice of human hurt. The first ice o
man hurt. The first ice of human hurt. The first ice of human hurt. The fir
human hurt. The first ice of human hurt. The first ice of human hurt. The
of human hurt. The first ice of human hurt. The first ice of human hurt.
the first ice of human hurt. The first ice of human hurt. The first ice of hum
rt. The first ice of human hurt. The first ice of human hurt. The first ice o
man hurt. The first ice of human hurt. The first ice of human hurt. The fi
human hurt. The first ice of human hurt. The first ice of human hurt. The
of human hurt. The first ice of human hurt. The first ice of human hurt.
the first ice of human hurt. The first ice of human hurt. The first ice of hum
rt. The first ice of human hurt. The first ice of human hurt. The first ice o

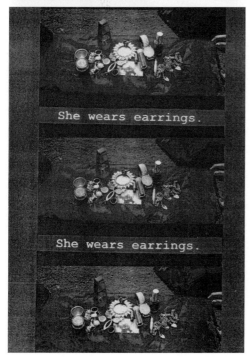

She wears earrings.

She wears earrings.

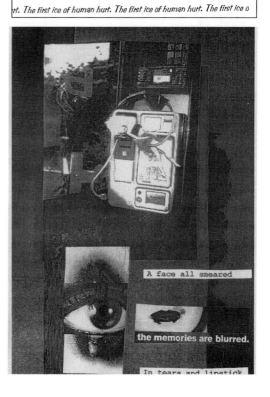

A face all smeared

the memories are blurred.

In tears and lipstick

Figure 2.5

Figure 2.5 (cont'd)

Task

Stage 1

Study the photostory called 'First Ice' (Figure 2.5). It is a reworking of a poem which some of you may have studied in GCSE English. It was presented by a group of GCSE Media Studies students at Cardiff High School (Hanna Truran, Anna Macey and Lumar Amaer).

Explore how the students who produced this have used mise-en-scène, captions, montage and special techniques in each of the panels.

Stage 2

Open out a poem or song of your choice using visual techniques.

Tips

1. Explore the title for content and themes.
2. Examine the poem or song line by line. Is there a basic narrative structure or theme running through? Can you work out a narrative formula?
3. The characters. Is there a narrator from whose point of view the poem is told? Are there any other characters mentioned? What are they like, do you think? Can you visualise them?
4. What is/are the setting(s)? Do you have visual suggestions for these?
5. What techniques will you use ? Photos: cut up or take? Will you use montage? Will you use the lines? Will you repeat lines in different ways? Will you add features other than photos? Will you use colour or black and white or both?
6. What kind of an audience would you have for such a production? Would it appeal to an audience who would not normally be interested in photostories?

Part 2: Investigating the 'docu-scape'

> ' I am a camera with its shutter open, quite passive, recording, not thinking.'
> Christopher Isherwood in 'Goodbye to Berlin'

Information

- The representation of events, ideas, people and places has to deliver a **point of view**.

- The point of view depends on the **relationship to the audience** the media product appeals to.
- There are many different types of representations of 'real' events, ideas, people and places.
- They are based on 'facts' about a subject (they are based on real people) or issue (they are real places) but **construct narratives, interpretations or comments** about the 'reality' of what is portrayed.
- These constructions can be 'informative', 'persuasive' and/or 'entertaining'.
- Representations of the world of real events and people are often controversial in terms of accuracy, truth, bias and objectivity.
- Through these representations we learn a lot about the world. They can change the ways we think about our lives and the lives of those around us by offering us viewpoints on important issues.

Activity

Docu-genres.

Extra information

- 'Genre' is the media term which allows you as a media student to classify or categorise the huge variety of docu-formats available to you as a modern viewer.
- Docu-formats have repeatable elements which you will recognise and allow you to predict the type of narrative.
- These elements have enormous importance in attracting an audience in the first place, especially in the age of the 'channel zapper'.
- Once the audience is 'hooked' they offer predictable patterns or structures but often with a new twist or variation. This both attracts viewers familiar with the product and new viewers to the product. Most docu-formats have a predictable narrative pattern. When they do not have this, they tend to be regarded as 'experimental' and often cause controversy.
- Genres mix with other kinds of genres to create new cross-over hybrid forms for an ever-demanding audience.
- Most genres have their 'fans' who know the history of the genre.
- Genres change and adapt as media producers compete for the audience.
- Many new television organisations do not use docu-formats.

Task 1: Docu-formats

Stage 1

Study the selected list of docu-formats in Figure 2.6. It is taken from a listings page about 'factual' programmes in a publication from the Christmas period in 1999 called *TV & Satellite Christmas*.

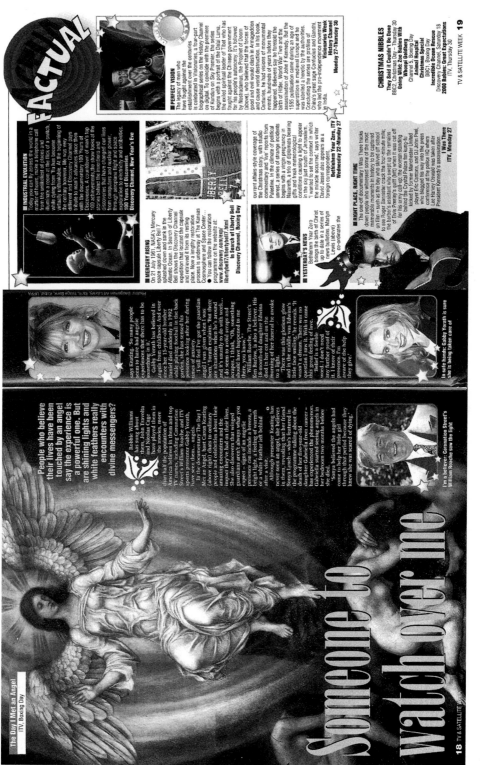

Source: TV and Satellite Week, *IPC Magazines*

Figure 2.6

Stage 2
Classify the list from the title and description using the following categories:
- informative;
- persuasive;
- exposing;
- amusing;
- witnessing;
- shocking.

Make a note of significant disagreements. Add other types you know of.

Tip
Listings magazines have the important functions of informing and attracting the audience. They are full of audience cues.

Task 2: The central elements of documentaries
Pick a docu-format of your own choice.

Tip
It does not matter if it is popular, entertaining or serious.
Use Table 2.2 to help you to identify the main elements of the media construction.

Observation	
What does the camera point at and record?	
What is the basis of its selection?	
Interviews	
Does the interviewer appear (on or off screen)?	
Do they interact?	
Do the interviewees speak for themselves?	
How are the interviews 'edited'?	
Dramatisation	
Does the observation allow you to be witness to dramatic events?	
How is dramatic conflict created?	
Is there a central character or group?	
Who is the central character or group up against?	
Is there 'a resolution' or does the observation create an 'open' ending which poses further questions?	
Does the producer use 'reconstructions'? (Material, as in photostories, where you used a script and actors dressed to play parts.)	

Mise-en-scène	
How are the shots composed?	
Exposition	
What is the main point?	
What is the purpose of the production and what is it trying to say?	

Table 2.2

Extra information

● **Undercurrents** is a co-operative of media producers which was set up in the 1990s to challenge the mainstream approach to production.

● It aims to attract an audience who want to know about the news, current affairs, advertisements and documentaries you do not see in mainstream films and on mainstream television.

Task 3

Read the article in Figure 2.7. List 10 things you have learned about the organisation.

Task 4: Interview with a documentary media producer

Read the transcript of a section of an interview with Helen Iles who produced a video about a small South Wales community.

Tip

A transcript is a written-down version of speech.

As you read, text-mark the points where she deals with the main elements of documentary.

Q. *I was wondering if we could move on slightly to describe some of the work you have been doing with Undercurrents, because you mentioned that you have made a change in what you were doing. What motivated that change?*

A.   The connection with Undercurrents came about through some filming I was doing at an area in Swansea called Holtsfield, which was undergoing pressure from a landlord to evict a group of families from a community, and I knew some people who lived there and I just went down with a camera whenever something kicked off and thought it was important to document it. I didn't really understand any of the issues that were going on there, I just knew that it was important. So it was, if you like, news and documentary again completely interfering with my private life, my working life and everything, but I would just stand there every moment I could, filming it.

At the end of two years I had masses of footage and I didn't know what to do with it. I hadn't organised it into any sort of film, I didn't know what audience, I didn't know what to do with it. And then I met somebody from Undercurrents who said 'We have had an eye on this case for three years and we have been looking for a programme'.

Q.   *A little bit about the case – I mean I'm very familiar with it but I think a lot of people . . .*

A.   About Holtsfield? It was about a group, a community, of people living in wooden chalets which had been been there, built between the wars for people to come and escape from the city, and they had built a community there over 20, 30 years and there were now 20-odd families living there, and then someone bought the land from underneath them and kicked them off. And wanted to build executive housing and so there were so many issues.

As I made a film over the two years I kept on thinking 'Oh it's about access to land and how we all have a right to access to land, we all have a right to our little plot and we shouldn't have to pay a fortune for it' and then it was about the exclusivity of being able to pay for that and why should it be executive homes and not little wooden chalets and then it was about the historical relevance of the wooden chalets and that they should be preserved and oh, it was about so many different things. Basically, they are still there.

Q.   *So how in the end did you decide to focus? You had lots of different kinds of approaches in the kind of film footage. How did you decide to organise it in the end?*

A.   Undercurrents helped me to focus it because Undercurrents said 'It is a campaign video'. And what Undercurrents do is that they go into a situation like that where people are struggling against something, they have an agenda of human rights and environmental awareness, so wherever those kinds of issues are brought up they will make a campaign video to promote awareness for the people who are having the problem. Usually there is no money involved, they don't have a lot of money, they just need help and they need to get their issues into the mainstream media.

Often they are issues that are ignored by the mainstream media, so they are finding it very difficult to get their point of view promoted. And often the

Candid camcorder

Undercurrents videos show the angles television news misses

Simon Hattenstone

BONG! Police disperse M11 road protesters with undue force. Bong! Criminal Justice Act outlaws peaceful protest. Bong! "Unemployable" man makes living pulling dropped coins out of drain. And finally! Third Word countries silenced as Gatt destroys millions of jobs and paves way for environmental disaster.

It may not be what Trevor McDonald had in mind, but Undercurrents is good news for the British media. The alternative news service is produced on video cassette and is available by mail order or from independent book shops. Dedicated to environmental and social justice issues, its philosophy is simple – place the Hi8 camcorder (best quality) in politically sensitive situations, give time to people not normally heard, show angles not normally seen, and continue filming even when the nice man with the badge puts his hand over the lens.

After Channel 4's initial radical surge, many alternative documentary film-makers felt they lacked an outlet. Thomas Harding, one of six members of Small World, the non-profit-making media company that runs Undercurrents, found he could not get his environmental films shown. Distributors would tell him they were too political, that they needed re-angling.

Sorry, he would reply, but they *are* political and that *is* the angle.

Harding joined forces with Jamie Hartzell, another environmental film-maker. They started Undercurrents to enable Small World to report the issues and events that, but for a riot, would go unnoticed, and to encourage grass-roots direct action.

The first issue (the second comes out this month) was impressive. It ran at 85 minutes, cost £4,000 to make and was shot by a mix of activists and Small World workers. The quality was surprisingly good, but it didn't really matter; often the filming was at its most powerful when at its shakiest. With no presenters, just a string of films accompanied by subtitle readbites, the format is almost Chart-Showish.

Undercurrents shocks (we see houses pulverised with people barricaded inside), informs (on the Criminal Justice Act) and exposes (the Bash The Baddy spot fires politically embarrassing questions at figures or authority till they go red). The profile of the drainer who makes a living from recovering dropped coins is funny, sad and strangely uplifting. Its 40-minute documentary on the M11 road protesters, filmed long before they hit the mainstream news, won first prize at Germany's Okomedia film festival. "We tried to sell this to British TV

stations, but they all said it was unusable," says Harding.

The camcorder has long been associated with Beadlesque inanity, but Undercurrents proves it to be a wonderful enabling tool. A vital part of Small World's work is training volunteers to make decent films. "The availability of high-quality video means that professionals are not the only ones who can make programmes," says Harding. Nevertheless, the BBC has recently equipped its professional foreign reports with camcorders so they can turn radio's From Our Own Correspondent into television.

While the camcorder is unlikely to transform mainstream news, it can *make* the news, as with the recording of Los Angeles police beating Rodney King, and can also challenge normal news values. Increasingly, the media is having to revise its original reporting of conflicts as people come forward with video evidence that contradicts their stories.

Although Undercurrents has received an EU grant, it is hardly rolling in riches (Small World members pay themselves £125 a week). But it can afford a certain insouciance. With next to no assets it does not fear libel suits, and is prepared to name names and, if necessary, secretly tape and broadcast conversations.

Despite its promising start, Under-

currents could struggle. With only three issues a year planned, topicality will be difficult. And at close on £10, (for the employed), Small World does not reckon on selling more than 1,000 copies of the early issues. But only viewers have passed on the message – and video – it estimates that up to 100,000 people could get to see it.

Then there is the age-old problem: how do you make yourself known to those who are not already converted to the cause? One way forward is to tackle a broader range of issues. It also hopes to reach a wider audience by placing "shorts" in sympathetic cinemas and selling individual items to national and local TV stations.

Actually, Undercurrents would sit easily and proudly in the medium for the masses, but TV has never been quite as democratic as it likes us to believe, not even in the days when the BBC cuddled up to Ken Loach, or when Channel 4 darned the socks of any documentary film-maker who could spell "anti-establishment". Anyway, if television were to set aside a nice little slot for alternative news, wouldn't it implicitly involve a terrible admission – that its perfectly balanced accounts of events just may have been skewed in the first place?

The Guardian
5 December 1994

Figure 2.7

mainstream media will be on the opposite side, so it is about promoting ideas ... that aren't out there and getting them out there through using camcorders. Under*currents* work through camcorders. It encourages people to go and film their own situations and make films from their own points of view.

Q.   *So what kind of a narrative came out?*

A.   The narrative focused on their struggle. It focused on what means they'd taken to actually fight the developers who wanted to take their land off them and develop it. It got a lot into the filming of the direct action: tree dwellers and the tunnel dwellers came into it because some of those techniques have been used at Holtsfield when the evictions came about.

Q.   *So how did they then seek to publicise what they had been doing within the mainstream media as well as a record?*

A.   The mainstream media did come in and do a piece. It wasn't very ... it was a lifestyle piece, basically. It was saying 'Oh, isn't it cutsey to live here' and 'Oh, what a shame, never mind'. It wasn't actually trying to make a change and Under*currents*' mission statement is to use video as a tool for social change by changing attitudes and by getting other voices out there into the mainstream.

Q.   *Did this determine the kinds of voices you used?*

A.   Well, I used the voices of the residents that lived there. We did a series of interviews and the interviews created the narrative, so it was done wholly from the point of view of the people who lived there.

There is quite a long-standing tradition of recording participants and editing them into narrative. It was a conscious decision not to use the 'voice of God'. We didn't want a narrator to guide the audience through the understanding of this case. We wanted the people to speak for themselves, we wanted them to hear their voices.

Q.   *When it got to the editing process, did it cause any problems?*

A.   Yes, tremendous problems, yes. We had to redo interviews all over the place because we would go to put the story together and we would discover there was a bit of the story missing and in a normal mainstream production house, you would voice it over. The voice-over ties together the whole film and holds it together. It is not that Under*currents* never uses those techniques, but I was particularly keen not to, so I had to keep on going back and get people to tell me that bit of the story again so that we could use it.

Q.   *So has the involvement of Undercurrents changed the way that you practise?*

A.   Yes, I am far more aware of the way that the media changes attitudes and opinions – how powerful it is. I am far more aware of how powerful the media is and far more aware of how to use that to manipulate public opinion all the time.

Task 5: Making your own documentary: research, planning and narrative

Stage 1: Research: Choose the topic
- Make it close to your concerns about something.
- Choose something on which you have a point of view.
- Do you want to entertain as well as inform?
- Find out all you can about it, from a variety of sources.
- Pick your witnesses or experts.

Stage 2: Format: Choose the style
- Do you want to use a **voice-over** to anchor the visuals?
  (Often called the '**voice of God**' style.)
- Do you want to rely on the pictures to tell the story and let the speakers tell their stories? This style is called **cinema-verité**. The camera operator acts as a '**fly-on-the-wall**'.
- Will you mix approaches using observation, interview and voice-over to get your point of view across?
- Will you draw attention to the fact that the people involved know they are being filmed by speaking and directly interacting with the film-maker? This is described as a '**self-reflexive**' approach.

Stage 3: Approach: The narrative
- What is the '**initial situation**' which the narrative seeks to create '**a resolution**' for or pose questions about or demand action on?
- What is the problem posed?
- Who/what opposes?
- Who/what offers solutions?
- What should the viewer do or how should they respond?

Stage 4: Shoot and evaluate: Record your footage
The 10 most common mistakes when shooting video:
1. Running out of batteries.
2. Videoing when you don't mean to (for example, shots of walking feet) and not videoing when you do (for example, leaving the camera on standby).
3. Too much **zoom** and **pan**.
4. Videoing from a distance with zoom close-up, so that the image is wobbly.
5. Composing a shot with too much sky/space above the subject.
6. Accidentally switching on a digital effect.
7. Missing the action because you're videoing something else at the time.

8. Recording with the date on.

9. Switching off the camera too quickly after the action has stopped.

10. Failing to think how the footage will be distributed.

(Source: Thomas Harding, *The Video Activist Handbook* (Pluto Press).)

Stage 5: Editing: The most challenging, time-consuming bit

- You are asking yourself questions about which shots, order of shots, titles, graphics, music, length.
- They are all to do with the basic purpose of your work: are you entertaining, informing or persuading your target audience?
- Editing is where all the creative decisions are made.
- Technology is speeding the process up but it does not change the amount of creative thought needed.

1. Access to technology is crucial here. The cost of technology is one of the central issues when the media are studied.

Methods of editing

Camcorder-VCR
Most of you will be able to access this method. You will need: • your video footage; • a blank VHS tape; • a VHS player.
Two-machine
You will need: • a video player; • a recorder; • two television monitors; • an edit suite.
Non-linear
You will need: • computer hardware; • image-editing software.

Table 2.3

2. Transfer your footage to a format where it can be edited.
3. Log your material and evaluate it for quality.
    - Summarise content as a list.
    - Describe content in sections (type of material, type of shot).
    - Time sections in minutes and seconds.
    - Make comments on quality and ideas for improvement.
4. Reorganise the footage into sequences. Refer back to your ideas about the narrative (**conflict, confrontation, angle**); **initial situation, development, resolution (open/closed)**.
5. Make a paper edit.
    - Identify the shots you will use in the order in which you use them.
    - Identify where the material is.
    - Transfer the times.
    - Describe the shots.
    - Make notes on the audio elements.
6. Edit. Have a number of efforts at this. Make notes on key decisions taken.
    Three ways of editing shots:
    - Cutting by scene: in one location and at one time.
    - Parallel cut: two or more locations.
    - Montage.

    (Adapted from *Oxford Film and Video-Makers*, Richard Herring)
7. Make a rough-cut. Show it to a selected audience and listen to their suggestions. Evaluate their responses.
8. Make an edit decision list. What's in and what out? You will need an evaluation meeting.
9. Evaluate the final edit. Quality criteria:
    - poor sound;
    - frames with spaces between (flash frames);
    - sloppy cuts;
    - out-of-focus images;
    - too much panning and zooming;
    - no clear narrative structure.

Activity

The Rodney King case.

- This was a really important issue for media activists using camcorders.
- It raises a complex set of issues to do with the use of the camcorder as 'evidence'.

Task

Stage 1
Study the comic book version of the case in Figure 2.8.

Stage 2
Discuss the issues it raises about the camcorder. Many of these can be developed from your work on the still image and the issues to do with editing video documentary work.

Stage 3
Study media programmes (especially on television) which use 'evidence' as 'entertainment' (for example, 'You've Been Framed').

Stage 4
Study media programmes on television which use 'evidence' as 'information' and 'entertainment' (for example, 'Drivers From Hell', 'Driving School').

Figure 2.8

134

Figure 2.8 (cont'd)

3 MEDIA ORGANISATIONS: ENTERTAINMENT

Inside the House of the Mouse: Team Disney

Look at Figure 3.1.

Information

● As a consumer in Great Britain you will not have escaped Disney. Twentieth-century audiences all over the globe have been part of the incredible growth of a media

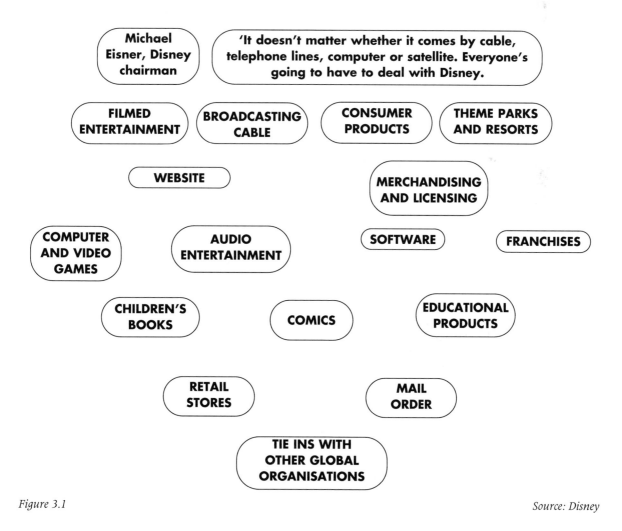

Figure 3.1

Source: Disney

company which started out 'with a mouse', as Walt Disney was fond of reminding his employees.

- Disney is a global organisation whose entertainment products are sold and distributed all over the world.
- Disney comics and the characters in them reach even the most remote parts of the world. Nearly everyone has heard of Mickey, Donald and Goofy, even in places where there is no television or cinema or phones and no Internet access.

Why is Disney important to study?

- It is an example of a **global conglomerate** which markets media products like books, music, movies, television and film to a mass audience.
- It creates 'wants' for consumers. The experience of a film or comic creates a further desire to own the video, the key chain, the computer game, the fluffy toy, the pyjamas, the pen and pencil set, and so on.
- It has extended the range of its operations into theme parks in various parts of the world, into 'fantasy worlds' which promise entertainment and at the same time market goods to the consumer. It offers the chance to escape into 'the magic' of the Disney world.
- It ties in its operations with other powerful global companies like McDonalds.

Disney values: 'Imagineering' and the Theme Park.

Extra information

- 'Imagineering' is a purely Disney word. It represents the collision of art and science.
- It combines 'engineering' with 'ideas and images' to create a 'themed' park.
- It represents a partnership of designers (ideas and images), developers (makers and builders) and marketing people (selling and promoting).

Activity   **Theme park advertising.**

Task 1

Discuss your class's experiences of theme parks. Study brochures about Disney theme parks.

- What promises do they make? Does this match the experience?
- What kinds of pictures of people and places are there in the brochures?
- What characters or settings do you recognise?
- Do certain colours predominate?

Task 2
Read the following quotation:

> 'As you can imagine, an unparalleled spectrum of opportunity awaits. From the grandest plans for major attractions, hotels and whole new cities to the tiniest elements like light fixtures, restaurant menus, wallpaper and trashcans – every detail will be created by this combined team of imagineers.'
>
> Michael Eisner

Make suggestions for road signs which will guide the visitor to a new Disney theme park. (Assume that it will be located somewhere in your region or country.)

General tips
There are three main kinds of sign:
● Large roadway signs announcing how near you are.
● Message signs: 'Tune your car into Disney World's exclusive radio channel'. Advertisements for products.
● Direction markers: 'Turn left, right in x metres'.

Think about:
● ways of visually 'teasing' the occupants of the car so that they felt they were getting nearer and nearer;
● use of colour;
● typeface;
● famous Disney **icons**.

Task 3: Disney values.
Look at Figure 3.2

Stage 1
Read the quotations from a variety of people about Disney theme parks.

Stage 2
Text-mark words/phrases that have connotations of key Disney values.

Stage 3
Make them into a spider diagram with Disney at the centre.

"Walt Disney dreamed of a place where families could go to have fun together – a place of fantasy and magic. Disneyland was the first of many such places and Imagineering is where the real magic is created. I believe it is the most magical organization in the world."

— MICHAEL D. EISNER

"Any ride engineer can design parts. But it is a unique kind of engineer who can blend a creative story and theme with practical technology. To continue to rise to the standard-setting challenge as a ride engineer here, you have to be more than a nuts and bolts type of person. You have to be a big thinker, a 'blank sheet of paper' person."

— DON HILSEN

Thanks to their dreams, themes, and magical schemes, the world is a happier place. Since the sun never sets on a Disney theme park, someone is smiling, laughing, singing, learning, caring, uniting, even forgetting about their most serious of worldly cares, even as you read these words. At this very moment, regardless of age, they are happily being swept away like a child in the magical embrace of a wondrous place created by those who build castles in the air as well as on the ground.

Michael D. Eisner
Chairman and CEO
The Walt Disney Company

"Walt Disney Imagineering is a true Renaissance organization. The only people I see who are successful at changing the world are right here – people with very special dreams."

— RAY BRADBURY

"All I want you to think about is when people walk through or have access to anything you design, I want them, when they leave, to have smiles on their faces. Just remember that. It's all I ask of you as a designer."

— WALT DISNEY

Shovels are turning in a passionate yearning for earth to meet our dream. Soon, we begin to manifest the idea in brick, mortar, steel, glass, wood, and paint. When the elements are assembled in a magical place, they define the shape of enchantment. They build the dream.

"I don't want the public to see the world they live in while they're in the park. I want them to feel they're in another world."

— WALT DISNEY

"To be sure all of the colors would work well with the new action occurring on the scene, Walt would send us to the park twice a month to identify possible color problems and to make adjustments accordingly. Some of the changes were quite subtle, but they were made nonetheless."

— JOHN HENCH

"Engineers everywhere are problem solvers. In this respect, we are no different than outside engineering firms that design and build complex projects like oil refineries. But at Imagineering, there's something about the nature of what we do and our unique product that makes our jobs more challenging, interesting and fun."

— ART HENDERSON

Figure 3.2   *Source:* Walt Disney Imagineering: A Behind the Dreams Look at Making the Magic Real, *Hyperion Books, 1998*

Activity   **Representations of heroes, heroines and villains in the animated films.**

Additional information
- Animation always draws attention to the construction of representations.
- You will be asking questions about the typicality of the functions of these standard characters in the animated films.
- Remember, they will be easily identified, will have simplified characteristics and will be recognisable for what they are in the film.

Task 1

Stage 1
List five Disney heroes. For each one produce a spider diagram of their main identifying features.

Stage 2
List five Disney heroines. For each one produce a spider diagram of their main identifying features.

Stage 3
List five villains (male or female). They usually have features which contrast with those of the heroes and heroines. These kinds of opposition are at the basis of the dramatic conflict in the stories. Test this idea further.

Tip
Use the following aspects of *mise-en-scène*:
- Facial representations: hair, eyes, smile.
- Body representations: ways of walking, hands, physical handicaps, non-American facial features, ability to change shape/morph.
- Costumes/clothes representations: typical colours, contrast of simplicity and extravagance.
- Sound representations: ways of talking (accents, lisps, use of complex words), associated music and sound effects.

Task 2: Typical ways of telling the story

Extra information
- Disney animations are full of Disney values. In particular, the stories are constructed to represent the triumph of good over evil.
- Main characters are established at the beginning of the film.
- Their world is disrupted in some way or threatened.
- They embark on a journey/quest to recover what has been lost.

- It is a quest full of tests and trials which 'teach' the central characters something about the world.
- The story ends when normality is restored with the promise of a brighter, more secure future. Endings are optimistic.

Stage 1

Using six to nine frames only, illustrate the narrative of a typical Disney film. Use speech bubbles, captions and the typical representations shown in the film.

Stage 2

Compare your drawn stories of different films to add to the above information about typical narratives.

Tip

Trace the characters from any publicity material about the film (video covers, posters).

Or scan such material and edit the images chosen .

Activity   **Studying Disney productions.**

Extra information
- The examples are taken from two different periods of Disney. 'Beauty and the Beast' is a Disney classic. 'A Bug's Life' and 'Toy Story' are recent productions. 'Toy Story 2' is even more recent.
- You can use the work you do to test whether Disney values have remained the same.

Beauty and the Beast   *Source: Walt Disney Co*

'Beauty and the Beast'.

Task 1
Make notes with a partner on these aspects of the film:

- the first 10 minutes of the film;
- the last 10 minutes;
- identify the problem posed in the opening;
- do the Beast and Belle make different journeys? What does each of them 'learn'?;
- what elements of the film are repeated? (Tips: Music, colours, camera shots and angles, set design);
- how is time handled in the film? (Tips: How does the film suggest the passing of time? How important is the beginning on our sense of the film's time? Does the sense of time add to the dramatic tension of the film?)
- what other kinds of typical films can you identify in this film? (Tips: Romance, horror, musicals.) List the elements;
- use the technique of spider diagrams to make notes on the main characters. How typical are they?;
- list some of the main audience cues which will help you identify the audience for the film.

Task 2
Give a close analysis of the film to show how it has been constructed. Try to explain why this 'old' film can still appeal to a 'modern' audience.

'A Bug's Life', 'Toy Story' and 'Toy Story 2'.

ABug's Life   *Source: Walt Disney Co*

Task 1
Construct a simple survey to discover which was the more popular film. Consider:

- best-loved male character;
- best-loved female character;

- favourite sequence;
- most-loved voices;
- best-dressed character;
- favourite or most memorable lines;
- best joke;
- best 'tear-jerking' moment;
- best bit of 'nail biting' stuff.

Toy Story   *Source: Walt Disney Co*

Task 2

List the attributes common to the heroes and villains of each of the films.
- Start with spider diagrams of each.
- Work out a way of linking the attributes together.

Task 3

Study the narratives of each film. How typical are they?
- Identify the hero as **A**.
- The villain as **B**.
- **C** their first meeting and the start of the problem.
- **D** the resolution of the problem.
- **E** as the outcome.
- Link **A**, **B**, **C**, **D** and **E** into a sequence.
- Test whether this simple structure works.

Task 4

- Every Disney character, film, song and piece of music is licensed. This means that you cannot use it for any commercial purpose without the permission of the Disney corporation.
- Disney will let other companies make products which feature typical Disney characters and ideas. These companies have to pay Disney for the use of its materials and be licensed by it. Disney, therefore, has control

of merchandising. It is one of the toughest companies in the world for the protection of its 'name'.

- Disney merchandising has been one of the most important successes for Disney in terms of making money and reinforcing its brand identity and core values.

- Many companies offered their products for use on the screen for 'Toy Story 2'. This is called **'product placement'**. It is a very common feature of American films and there are American companies who specialise in advising other companies on the best ways to get the products featured in film productions.

Read the following short extract from 'Buzz, Woody ... and Barbie plays too' which appeared in the *Observer* in December 1999 (Figure 3.3). What issues does it raise about 'product placement'?

Previously sceptical toy manufacturers, encouraged by the critical acclaim lavished on the original *Toy Story*, came forward to offer their products for use on screen. Mattel, for example. When *Toy Story* made its debut in 1995, there was bemusement about the characters that were missing from the action. Aside from its fictional heroes – strident plastic space ranger Buzz Lightyear and folksy cloth cowboy puppet Woody – there were plenty of recognisable playroom favourites: Mr Potato Head, Slinky Dog, Barrel of Monkeys, Etch-A-Sketch. But where was Mattel's Barbie, a twentieth-century icon and America's favourite doll?

The answer is that Mattel has reservations about the script. Barbie was envisaged as an ultra-feminine Sigourney Weaver-type action woman who, at a crucial point in the storyline, would roar up in a pink Corvette and party dress, order the toys into the car and drive them to safety. This was not acceptable to Mattel, which, according to *Toy Story* director John Lasseter, 'believed that little girls, when they play with Barbie, make up the personality of the toy. They didn't want us to

say, "When Barbie comes alive, she's like this".'

'We wanted to have Barbie in the first film very badly,' confirms Ash Brannon, the sequel's co-director. 'Mattel thought it was up to girls who played with Barbie to determine who she was. But then they saw how well *Toy Story* turned out and how true we were to the real toys...'

The upshot makes for a significant scene in the new movie. Woody has been kidnapped by a greasy collector of rare toys, who recognises him as an item from the Fifties, and Buzz Lightyear is leading an assault on Toy Barn, the massive toy superstore where he thinks Woody is being held. Buzz gets separated and stumbles on an aisle where shelves are piled to the roof with Buzz Lightyear dolls, strapped into their identical packaging, soulless and mass-produced. Meanwhile Ham, the pink plastic piggy bank, is driving a blue toy pick-up truck around the aisles when suddenly he and others hear the stirring sounds of the Surfaris' 'Wipe Out' played Hawaiian-style. Turning a corner, they are confronted by a vast army of Barbies enjoying a lavish pool-

side party, chatting and laughing, dancing the twist and the limbo. In contrast to the uniformly dour Buzz Lightyear collection (four years on, the only new feature is a utility belt), there are dozens of differently dressed and coloured Barbies, and in a scene perhaps adapted from the first movie's original script, one jumps into the truck with the toys. She is, she informs them, Tour Guide Barbie and, after asking them all to strap in safely, politely asks Mr Potato Head to keep all his removable body parts inside the vehicle.

Mattel's eagerness to sign up doesn't so much reflect opportunism as satisfaction that *Toy Story 2* is low-risk. Barbie – who celebrated her fortieth birthday this year – remains one of the biggest-selling dolls in history and the company claims that sales worth $1.7 billion were made last year alone. The doll remains its flagship product and an attempt to transfer Barbie know-how to the software market came unstuck this year, when the company failed to match predicted profits and suffered a slump in its share price.

Observer
December 1999

Figure 3.3

Toy Story 2   *Source: Walt Disney Co*

Activity   'Toy Story': Another way of looking.

Extra information

- Another way of looking at Disney productions is to consider that they offer massive marketing opportunities for the company. Some people suggest that this is the real importance of the films and theme parks.
- Other critics point to the way in which Disney values are typical American values which are exported all over the globe.

Task 1: Genre

Stage 1
What features of the beginning of the film 'brand' it as a Disney film?

Stage 2
How many representations of the cowboy western hero can you find in Woody?

Stage 3
What signs are there of changes in Woody's function in the way in which Andy uses him prior to opening Buzz?

Stage 4
List the signs which associate Buzz with science fiction film.

Adding to the working definition: Iconography
This refers to typical signs (and therefore signs which have a history), whose meanings have become fixed through regular and conventionalised usage. All

openings of media texts are significant, as they are an important aspect of their selling point and can clearly be linked to posters and publicity.

Adding to the working definition: Genre
Genre is concerned with the relationship between the text and the audience. This raises further key issues about industrial production, distribution strategies, marketing and exhibition.

The concept of genre as a set of typical signs is important as a point of departure for the audience: it points not only to the knowledge the audience is assumed to have, but also to the work the audience has to do.

Task 2

Stage 1
List the signs associated with some of the characters such as the soldiers, Mr Potato Head, Bo Peep.

Stage 2
a   Consider the signs that make Woody a politician.
b   Consider how the issue of his replacement is raised in a variety of ways.
c   Consider how Woody is set up as the stereotypical hero: the disruption, the journey, the tests, the helpers and the resolution.
d   Consider how Buzz also has to make a journey of self-knowledge.
e   Consider how other characters, such as Andy or Sid, face up to their fears.

Task 3

Explain briefly whether one or all these assertions is/are a valid way of looking at 'Toy Story':

- **Statement 1:** 'Bad' or selfish people will always get their 'come-uppance' and the truth will find everyone out.
- **Statement 2:** Everyone must be reconciled to the truth, however tough a process that is.
- **Statement 3:** Everyone must 'reach for the stars' and go 'to infinity and beyond'.

Task 4

Have you discovered other values embedded in the film that make you 'read' it differently from the first time you saw it?

4 MEDIA ORGANISATIONS: NEWS AND CURRENT AFFAIRS

Information

- Organisations providing news and comment on current affairs devote an immense amount of energy and an enormous range of resources to their production of news and current affairs.
- There is a cross-over from medium to medium in the kinds of skills and abilities needed by producers to keep audiences informed and up to date with developments in the world. The basics of telling a story are central to all media. However, the medium chosen affects the narrative (the way the story is told).
- All news and current affairs programmes need well-informed people who can think and respond quickly and have a wide-ranging set of interests. They will often have specialist knowledge of such things as local and national sport, the workings of politics or the economy or business or the arts and media, experience of different parts of the world, and so on.
- They quickly need to understand typical ways of constructing materials like reports, stories and features, whether written, as in newspapers, or live, as on radio or television.
- All media organisations have sets of 'values' which organise their stories and shape them for the audience. Often these are obvious in the way the organisation appeals to its core audience. Sometimes they are so much a part of the way in which programmes and newspapers are produced they feel like 'common sense', even to the producers.
- Many of the people who 'front' the news are media celebrities because of the quality of their work.
- Many of them diversify their media careers by crossing into other media genres and forms.

Why are news and current affairs productions important for media students?

- They raise key questions about 'truthful information' and its relationship to 'point of view'.
- They help to explain events in the real world.
- Because, in a highly competitive media world, the media need to be able to attract

audiences, the 1990s in particular have witnessed a whole set of media initiatives designed to attract them to news and current affairs productions.

● It is sometimes argued that the advent of electronic newspapers may revolutionise the newspaper industry and yet 1999 witnessed the birth of a new Sunday tabloid. This means that news and current affairs programmes and publications in the 1990s can help media students to explore the change of 'old' media (based on separate media) to 'new media'(based on the process of digitalisation).

● In doing so, it is often suggested, they may 'trivialise' important issues in a process called 'dumbing down'.

● They may also 'sensationalise' stories by looking for the most bizarre, titillating or shocking aspects.

Activity

The conventional newspaper feature.

Extra information

● These kinds of stories have typical patterns because the way in which they are organised is related to the production process.

● If a more newsworthy story comes along then a report may have to be cut completely or edited to fit.

● Space and number of words are main production issues.

● Such reports are edited from the end upwards.

● This job is the work of a sub-editor. Reports are fed in from local areas and information is edited into appropriate forms in different newspapers.

● They can be a more important story in some newspapers than others.

Task 1

Study the article about Stereophonics from the *Western Mail*, 11 December 1999 (Figure 4.1).

Start at the end. Taking off a paragraph at a time, reveal the structure of the piece.

Tips

In which parts of the report do you find:

● who, when, where, at what time?

● corroboration through quotation?

Can you work out where the reporter got her additional information to construct her report?

Edit it into a 200-word report without losing any essential information.

Stereophonics to net audience from Cwmaman to California

TONIGHT'S Stereophonics' concert at Birmingham NEC will be shown live on the Internet.

Tens of thousands of people are expected to log on for the gig, which is being screened by MediaWave.

The Cwmaman trio were recently named by *Q Magazine* as Best Live Act in the World Today.

The band said they were delighted the concert, part of their UK tour, was being shown on the Internet.

"I can't believe people will be able to watch us from Cwmaman to California at the same time," said lead singer Kelly Jones.

Chris Frampton, managing director of MediaWave, said, "The success of the music scene from Wales has been awesome over the last couple of years. This event will help the Stereophonics achieve their ambition to go global."

The concert goes online at 9pm on www.mediawave.co.uk;

www.stereophonics.co.uk; www.v2music.com and www.msn.com.

The Stereophonics have already played two sell-out gigs in Cardiff this week as part of the tour.

They will play two more concerts, which have both sold-out, at Cardiff International Arena next Thursday and Friday.

On New Year's Eve, they will be performing at the Cream nightclub in Liverpool. That concert is the last chance Stereophonics fans will get to see the band playing live in the UK for a while. It has been announced that the next concert they will play will be in the summer and probably part of a festival.

Meanwhile, the Manic Street Preachers have announced they will be releasing their new single on January 10.

The Masses Against the Classes will be the Blackwood band's first single since *Tsunami*, which was released in

July. But the new single is being described as a "stand alone" song, which won't be included on the follow-up album to *This Is My Truth Tell Me Yours*.

The group won't be making a video to accompany their new release, which was recorded in London in October.

Bassist Nicky Wire said, "We started the '90s with *Motown Junk* and we wanted to start a new decade with *The Masses Against The Classes*. It is a separate entity, a complete one-off, and has nothing to do with the next album."

The Manics are rehearsing for their concert at the Millennium Stadium in Cardiff on New Year's Eve.

A spokesman for the band said they would probably be touring America early next year.

The Western Mail
11 December 1999

Figure 4.1

Task 2
Produce the story as part of a news bulletin on your local radio station. Would the story have any other jobs to do on the early bulletins?

Tips
News bulletins are usually given on the hour and update the listener with what is going on in the world internationally, nationally and locally.

Activity The launch of a new Sunday tabloid.

Extra information
- The launch of a new tabloid newspaper at the end of 1999 suggests that there may be a place for the traditional newspaper in the new millenium.
- Its first edition suggests that the editors are aiming the tabloid at a new generation of highly educated people.

Task 1: Website
Study the homepage for the *planetonsunday* (Figure 4.2).

Figure 4.2

- ⊚ What are the connotations of the title?
- ⊚ How are these connotations reinforced in the graphics?
- ⊚ What promise does the slogan make? How typical is this?
- ⊚ How does the web page seek to personalise the audience?
- ⊚ Make a list of the 'values' on which the new publication is based.
- ⊚ How is it different to other tabloids? What makes it distinctive?

Task 2: Front pages
Look at the front page of the *planetonsunday* of 5 December 1999 (Figure 4.3).

Stage 1
Separate the main elements of the front page by cutting them up or tracing them.

Stage 2
Text-mark the key features of the front page of the first edition.

Tips
Use terms like 'masthead', 'trailing graphics', 'articles'.

How typical is the page in terms of layout?

THE planet*on*sunday

FIRST ISSUE 5 DECEMBER 1999   TOWARDS HEAVEN ON EARTH   50p

Behind the mystery of Hanger 18

UFO expert Nick Redfern reports on an other-worldly conspiracy

PAGES 22-23

Cure for cancer?
Brown rice extract may be the answer...PAGE 37

Mind over matter

Health writer Mo Elliot encourages readers to use that most powerful of tools, the mind, to realise our full potential

PAGE 40

DRIVE TO TIGHTEN GM DUMP CONTROLS

BY PRESTON WITTS

MINISTERS are to consider proposals to toughen the regulations governing the discharge of waste containing traces of GM material from factories and laboratories throughout Britain.

Campaigners are pressing for comprehensive monitoring of such discharges and for full public disclosure. Last Friday was the deadline for a hurriedly organised consultation period in which all those involved in the controversy were invited to submit their views.

The submissions will now be processed and a report sent to the government by the Health and Safety Commission before the end of January.

According to GeneWatch UK, an independent policy research group, releases of genetically modified micro-organisms (GMMs) are taking place, unmonitored, every day at sites all over the UK. GMMs are widely used for research purposes and by industry to produce drugs, enzymes and food additives.

A document prepared by GeneWatch, which was instrumental in prompting government action on the issue, states: "The use of GMMs could be on a huge scale. Although most waste is treated to kill the majority of organisms before it is disposed of, some living GMMs are still released."

It adds: "Extraordinarily, the Environment Agency, which is responsible for pollution control in the UK, has no information on where and how GMMs are being used in factories and therefore no knowledge of what GMMs are being released in waste streams or in serial discharges by the companies involved.

"The HSE (Health and Safety Executive), which is responsible for implementing the regulations covering the use of GMMs, conducts no monitoring and no enforceable levels of allowed pollution are established."

Dr Sue Mayer, director of GeneWatch UK, said: "We are working on this at a time when there is supposed to be freedom of information and open government. We are campaigning on the issue because we are concerned about public health, environmental safety and people's right to know."

Environment minister Michael Meacher is understood to have been genuinely surprised when he was informed about the lack of monitoring and comprehensive information about the discharge of GMMs. It was this revelation that convinced him of the need to dig out all the available facts and initiate a consultation process.

About 100 interested parties — including environmental groups, consumer organisations, industry associations and trades unions — were invited by the Health and Safety Executive to give their views.

Turn to page 2

Messages of hope from Diana's spirit

THE PLANET on Sunday launches today with the serialisation of Hazel Courteney's extraordinary book *Divine Intervention*, which tells of her dramatic near-death experience over Easter 1998 and her two-month possession by the spirit of Diana, Princess of Wales.

Hazel's life was turned upside-down on 8 April last year when she was struck by what felt like a thunderbolt in the famous London store Harrods. Strange phenomena began occurring to and around her and eventually Hazel found scientists who were able to explain how she was able to do seemingly impossible things.

The award-winning health columnist who met the Princess on several occasions believes that for more than six months she was communicating with Diana's spirit.

The hundreds of messages Hazel received include predictions about many of our possible futures, but also dire warnings of what could happen if we continue to neglect our health and that of our environment. We are aware that our decision to publish extracts from Hazel's book over the next five weeks will be perceived in some quarters as controversial and it is not our intention to upset or offend any readers. But saving our planet is about as serious a subject as can be found and we believe that the messages contained within this book need to reach as wide an audience as possible.

We hope you will agree.

Turn to pages 31-33 for the story.

www.planet-on-sunday.co.uk

Figure 4.3

Task 3: The news agency story
Look at the story in Figure 4.4.

Extra information

- This is a news agency story. It has been collected not by a newspaper reporter of the paper but by an agency which collects, edits and distributes news.
- The paper has paid the agency for the story by subscribing to its services.

Does it have a typical structure? How does it fit with the 'values' of the paper? Would other tabloids use this story in the same way?

'Leaky' GM crop warning

ENVIRONMENTAL campaigners sounded a warning after scientists shows that genetically modified corn leaked insecticide into the soil from its roots.

A fifth of the corn planted in the US last year was modified to produce an insecticide to protect itself against pests such as caterpillars.

According to the journal *Nature*, researchers at New York University found that the insect-killing toxin, called Bt, exudes from the plant's roots as well as the above-ground foliage and pollen.

A Greenpeace spokesman said: "This shows the ability of GM crops to constantly wrong-foot their creators and produce unexpected and unwanted effects...we have to ask why are we taking the risk?"

Figure 4.4

Welcome to ... The marketplace

As readers look through the Planet on Sunday they will not see large colourful advertising. Instead advertising will be confined to one section of the paper only. It will be restricted to what is known as 'classified advertising'.

This means that unless readers are particularly interested – perhaps thinking of buying a particular commodity or service – they need not read any advertising in order to enjoy the paper.

The Planet believes advertising should be a service to readers, and not part of the 'price' paid to read the newspaper's editorial content.

Such advertising is performing a proper economic function: it is giving consumers essential market information to enable them to make an informed choice in a free an competitive market place.

What such advertising does not do, is to try to persuade readers to want to buy something which, if they had not seen the ad, they would not have felt any need for.

The reason for this is that we at the Planet on Sunday believe that if we are to save planet earth – and this paper is about looking at ways in which we can all contribute – we must reduce our consumption of goods and services. To do this without reducing the quality of our lives it is necessary to avoid artificially stimulating our desire for things.

But there is another more immediate practical consequence of our decision to avoid advertising.

Many newspapers claim to be truly independent and state that their editorial content is not influenced by the advertising revenue they receive. This is not true, especially when big advertising agencies control several important clients – a newspaper or TV company will always consider the impact of their editorials on important customers.

We at the Planet on Sunday aim to be different. Our whole raison d'etre is to promote ideas for saving the planet.

Current levels of consumption are unsustainable and we hope that our approach to advertising will suggest one practical way forward.

Q. Why does the Planet on Sunday only carry classified advertising?

A. Because we feel that large display advertising throughout the paper would artificially stimulate our readers' desire for products which they do not want or need.

Q. Why advertise in the Planet on Sunday?

A. Because we are offering a specific service to the reader – a dedicated Marketplace to sell your product or service. The readers know where to find what they are looking for.

Figure 4.5

Task 4: Advertising
Look at Figure 4.5.

What different reasons are there for the use of advertisements in newspapers?

Collect your own examples and comment on the issues they raise for the consumer.

Task 5: Back page
Study the back page of the paper (Figure 4.6).

Identify one way in which it is similar to other tabloids. Identify one way in which it is different. Explain your reasons.

Task 6: Extended group task
Produce the front or back page of a tabloid newspaper for your local community.

Tips
- Decide on the appropriate 'values' and 'point of view' you will adopt. Evaluate different approaches through research.
- Agree an appropriate 'house style'. Evaluate different methods and approaches.
- Select **headlines**. Short? Sharp? Humorous? Evaluate and test in group sessions.
- Write your 'copy'. Follow the typical conventions for this. Make sure that you can edit the copy from the bottom upwards. It will help you with the layout.
- Select (or, better still, take) your photographs. Typical? Unusual angles? Evaluate in terms of 'news values'.
- Paste up your sample layout. Evaluate and test.
- Use whatever software you have available to produce the final copy.
- Evaluate your work in terms of 'typicality of approach' and new innovations you have used to attract the audience.
- Explain how you plan to distribute the first edition of the tabloid and the ways you will fund the production costs.

Activity   **Radio news reports: A simulation.**

Extra information
- Radio reports have the same main conventions as newspaper reports: identifying who, when, where, corroboration by eyewitnesses and quotes/interviews from experts, additional information to inform the viewer/listener.

planet*sport*

Bobsleigh Britons keep going for gold

BY RICHARD SYDENHAM

THE MOST exciting season in women's bobsleigh is now under way — and Great britain has high hopes of winning gold in at least one of the major championships in a two-man discipline.

The first stage of the World Cup was completed in Calgary, Canada, last week and although Britain's best placing was sixth, there was little more than a second between them and the winning American team.

It's too early to predict the likely medal winners, who will be finalised in Austria next february, but the brits will take heart from their bronze medal in last season's World Cup series, when they finished behind the USA and winners Switzerland.

The fact that the Federation of International Bobsleigh and Tobogganing (FIBT) scheduled the first women's World Championship for February 2000 in Winterberg, Germany, lends even greater interest to the season.

"It's a very exciting time for women's bobsleigh," said Cheryl Done, the driver of Britain's Team 2.

"We've wanted this for about eight years. To be told that we'll be in the 2002 Olympics in Salt Lake City as well is fantastic news.

"We've not been out of a medal position for five years so our medal hopes are looking very positive this season. However, we're still looking for more people to join the team, which will help us win the gold."

The FIBT only recognised women's bobsleigh two years ago, though their programme still existed unofficially. Britain were runners-up in the four years prior to last season, which is a remarkable achievement given the resources available to the sport here.

Henrietta Alderman, general secretary of the British Bobsleigh Association, said: "The sport is certainly still growing in this country.

"It's not easy to recruit people in to bobsleigh, although we are trying through universities and the services. Most of our team come from the Services — mainly the RAF — but we're now attracting athletes from track and field as well."

Done, from the Isle of Man, understands the difficulty in encouraging more people in to bobsleigh. "You're away from your normal job for four months of the year, training," she said. "I'm fortunate that the RAF give me the time off, but not everyone can get the time."

UK Sport provide the bulk of the money for British bobsleigh, as well as sponsors Adidas, Rover and a Yorkshire businessman.

These funds allow the team to prepare for the competitive season. Summer training consisted of fitness work like running and lifting weights as well as actual driving practice (on wheels) at Thorpe Park.

The women travelled to Lillehammer in Norway last month for on-ice training — a venue that is considered the Brits' home track. "Your preparation can be the difference between winning and losing a race," said Done.

"People think you do the sport in the winter months and that's it but there's a lot more to it than that.

"Personally, I've been on the brakes for five years so I had to get used to driving before embarking on the competitive season."

Britain are represented by Michelle Coy and Emma Merry in Team 1 and Vicky Stenson and Cheryl Done in Team 2.

The next stage of the World Cup series is in Lillehammer next January.

In the driving seat...Cheryl Done, of Britain's Team 2   PICTURE: CHARLIE BOOKER

Athletics bosses bid to inspire youth

MANY of today's youngsters, deemed unfit and more interested in computers than playing sport, will be targeted by UK Athletics in order to encourage health and fitness and improve the future of British athletics.

It is believed the current level of fitness among Britain's children is lower now than it has been for many years and it's an issue that the recently-formed UK Athletics body is seeking to put right.

"That's the big challenge for us at the moment," said Norman Brook, technical director for running events. "In the 1980s, UK athletics enjoyed its best times with the likes of Coe, Cram and Ovett.

"That was a time when you thought the sport couldn't be healthier, but in fact that was when the seeds of decline were being sown. Around 25 to 30 of our under-17 boys, who usually go on to form our future of endurance runners, could run the 1500 metres in less than four minutes in 1980.

"There was a steady decline throughout the 1980s and by 1998 we know that only two boys could do that. It's a huge fall in endurance running which has taken place over that period of time."

There are a multitude of reasons for the decline, ranging from more opportunities for children to do different types of sport or leisure pursuits; the fact that running is losing popularity amongst youngsters, and the growth of soccer.

"I suspect though," said Brook, "that a big part of it is lifestyle changes. Young people are not as fit as they used to be because they're not as active, and when they are active they don't seem to enjoy the activity as much as youngsters did in the past.

"These major cultural changes have had a massive impact on the health of young people, which in turn has had a major impact on the declining participation in sport."

So how do they plan to remedy this negative culture? Such a revolution will not happen over night, on the contrary. Injecting enthusiasm for sport — especially running — in to youngsters will not be an easy task when up against the tv and PlayStation.

"We don't have any initiatives yet as UK Athletics was only formed a year ago," Brook explained, "so what we're doing at the moment is developing a structure to re-establish everything and targeting our main priorities."

Cassie's chance to seize double glory

ENGLAND'S Cassie Campion, the current star of women's squash, goes into this week's British Open in Aberdeen as the number one seed — and victory will take the 26-year-old to the top of the world rankings, writes Richard Sydenham.

Australian Michelle Martin, ranked one in the world, dominated the sport for years by winning three World Opens and six British Opens, but she retired in October and Campion is now determined to emulate the 32-year-old Aussie.

"She's been the top player for the last few years and I'm just glad that I was able to beat her at the US Open and the World Open." said Cassie, the current world champion.

"The fact that Michelle won six British Opens in consecutive years just shows what a great champion she was. I'd love to win just one — never mind six!"

Despite current form, victory in the tournament — it starts tomorrow — is not a foregone conclusion for Campion, given a top quality field who will all be keen to stake their own claims for Martin's place at the top.

However, Campion is so happy with her game that she is brimming with confidence. The added incentive of topping the world rankings is another reason why her opponents may find her difficult to overcome.

"I feel that I have got a fantastic chance of winning the competition," she enthused. "All the players that are there I've beaten before, which is a boost for the confidence. If I play as well as I did in Seattle during the US Open there's no reason why I shouldn't win. I feel as though my squash improved by about 20 per cent in America.

"Obviously there's a lot more pressure on me now than usual being the top seed but I'm looking forward to it all the same. I am delighted that I have got up to second in the world and I'm just hoping that in January I will be number one.

"Becoming world champion was the main aim but now I've achieved that becoming number one in the world is another big target, on a par with winning the British Open."

She feels New Zealand's Leilana Joyce, seeded two, will be her main rival but acknowledges that Australian Carol Owens, England's Linda Charman and Natalie Grainger, of South Africa, will also be dangerous opponents.

Whatever the outcome in Aberdeen this week, the tournament will be Cassie's last of the year. She is looking forward to a rest over the Christmas period before resuming competition in the new year.

When the next world rankings are announced in January, it might be a moment for Campion to cherish. "I took up squash at nine years old, turned professional at 18, and it's been hard work to get where I am," she said. ""But when I think of all those junior tournaments, all the fitness training like running, hill sprints and gym work I've put in, it all seems well worth it now I'm world champion. To become number one in the world would be the icing on the cake."

ISSN 1363-9757

The Planet on Sunday is published by New Millennium Newspapers Ltd, Greville Court, 1665 High Street, Knowle, West Midlands B93 0LL and printed by Northcliffe Newspapers, Derby.

Figure 4.6

- There is more description than on television news where the pictures anchor the commentary. Radio reporters 'paint word pictures'.
- 'On the spot reporting' is a key component in all news media. Being in the right place at the right time is essential, though not always possible. Many reporters pride themselves on this ability.

Task 1

Stage 1
Read the following scenario very carefully:

Two animal rights activists have kidnapped a leading scientist, Dr John Peterson, at a scientific conference in a country house in Mid Wales. The conference had been organised by the medical research foundation Medi-ref and the drug company Feelwell.

It is understood that Dr Peterson and Feelwell were about to announce the development of a radical new drug for the treatment of skin cancer. It is also understood that Dr Peterson's research involved the use of rats, kittens, monkeys and mice. It is believed that the kidnappers belong to a radical group called Anima which has a record of violence and has been actively involved in the destruction of labs and the freeing of animals.

- The kidnapping took place at 8.30 this morning.
- Peterson was abducted from his car as he arrived at the Grand Hotel, Radnor.
- A spokesperson for the local police authority said they had received demands from the kidnappers but that only one of them involved a direct appeal on TV.

Stage 2
As a reporter you have access to:
1. A spokesperson for Anima (protesting outside hotel)
2. A spokesperson for Medi-ref (in the hotel as a guest)
3. An eyewitness at the Grand Hotel
4. The local MP (by phone)
5. The BBC's scientific correspondent (by live video link-up from your phone)
6. A patient from the local community suffering from skin cancer (researched from local newspaper office)
7. A government spokesperson (by phone)
8. An unidentified police source (non-attributable).

Task 2

Assemble a **running order** for a two-minute radio bulletin to be broadcast on the Twelve O'clock News from the BBC.

Tips

You will need to:

- script various parts of this;
- rehearse the people who play the various parts;
- use short sentences;
- juxtapose voices;
- have an authoritative and well-informed approach to the incident (BBC values);
- present a balanced view of the conflict (BBC values).

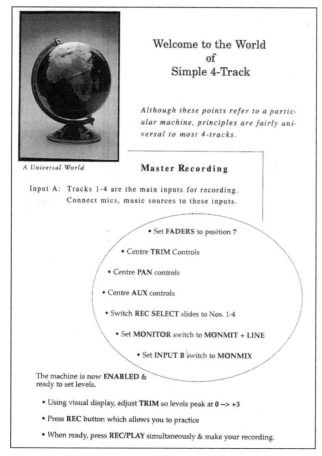

Welcome to the World
of
Simple 4-Track

*Although these points refer to a partic-
ular machine, principles are fairly universal to most 4-tracks.*

A Universal World

Master Recording

Input A: Tracks 1-4 are the main inputs for recording.
Connect mics, music sources to these inputs.

- Set **FADERS** to position 7
- Centre **TRIM** Controls
- Centre **PAN** controls
- Centre **AUX** controls
- Switch **REC SELECT** slides to Nos. 1-4
- Set **MONITOR** switch to MONMIT + LINE
- Set **INPUT B** switch to MONMIX

The machine is now **ENABLED** &
ready to set levels.

- Using visual display, adjust **TRIM** so levels peak at 0 –> +3
- Press **REC** button which allows you to practice
- When ready, press **REC/PLAY** simultaneously & make your recording.

Figure 4.7

Task 3

Record a 'live' version of the bulletin. Record your 'out takes'.

Tips

If you have access to and can use four-track editing it will help. See Figure 4.7.

Task 4 (individual)

Write up the task and evaluate the approach the group took.

Tips

- Explain your group's decisions. What was included and why? Significant disagreements? What personally would you have changed and why? Running order? Balance? Point of view?
- Was your broadcast the right length (to the second!!)? If not, where did it need editing?
- Use your 'out takes' to comment on the difficulties you had in selecting and presenting the material.
- Did your broadcast sound like a BBC bulletin? Why/why not?
- How would you change the bulletin for the Six O'Clock News from the BBC?

Activity Typical narrative structure of television news.

Task 1: Research: Identifying main elements
- Study two recorded bulletins from a mainstream television company such as BBC, ITV or Channel 5.
- Devise a flow chart for each programme.

Tips
- Opening sequence with signature tune and graphics
- The main stories in the running order
- Identifying the presenters and the stories
- Use of archive footage
- Use of outside broadcasts (live and recorded)
- Location interviews
- Video link-ups
- Summaries
- Trailing 'what's ahead'
- Sections with graphics embedded in them.

Task 2: Research: Analysing the opening sequence

Storyboard the opening.

Tip

After each frame is paused, draw what is in the frame and identify the sounds used.

Explain how each of the openings creates an impression of 'the news'.

Tips

- Voice-overs
- Music
- Graphics
- Studio sets
- Presenters: gender, ethnicity, appearance, style (serious/chatty), clothes, etc., behind/in front of news desk.

Task 3: Headlines and running orders

- Comment on the different headlines and the different organisation of the running order.
- How does this contribute to the creation of a varied and interesting programme in each case?
- Are all the stories of the same type?

Tips

Dramatic? Serious? Scandalous? Fun? Good news? Bad news? Tasters? Cliff hangers?

Task 4

- Select one story common to the two programmes.
- Identify differences in the way the story is told.

Tips

- Locations
- People for interviews
- Experts
- Witnesses.

Task 5

Comment on the closing sequences in each.

Tips

- Is it an 'open' or 'closed' ending?
- Is the music repeated?
- Same graphics used?

Activity **Planning a television news programme: A simulation.**

Extra information
You will need:

- a selection of newspapers from the same day;
- a video camera with a tripod;
- access to a photocopier (better still, an editing suite).

Task
Make a short news programme of between three and five minutes. It is aimed at the early evening audience on a new teenagers' channel.

Stage 1
Tips
Establish the channel identity. Give the television company a name and logo. Clearly establish its values by discussion.

More tips: Modern? Cool? Up to date? Zany?

Stage 2
From the newspapers choose five stories which will appear on your news programmes. Explain your choices in terms of the teenage audience.

Tips
Build in lots of audience cues: choice of presenters, style of set, approach to stories, etc.

Stage 3
Plan a running order.

Tips
- Clear sense of start. Snappy headlines which arouse curiosity and expectation.
- Most important/interesting story first.
- An item to round off.

Stage 4
Plan the production style.

Tips
As live footage is impossible, try the following:
- tape footage from a broadcast and anchor it with a voice-over (quite difficult!);
- select photographs from the newspaper stories, enlarge them on a photocopier and use them as stills behind the presenters.

PART 2
STUDYING MAJOR MEDIA INDUSTRIES

Working definition of 'media industry'

- A media industry is a system of production which uses people to make media products.
- Media industries use a wide range of technologies.
- The type of technology used affects the final production.
- The people employed in media industries have a range of training backgrounds and a wide variety of specialist skills.
- They use these skills and abilities to attract the largest possible audience to the media product.
- It is very hard work to attract the attention of the audience.
- Competition is very intense in the mainstream media industries.

Working definition of 'narrative'

Each media industry has a specialist 'language' to create narratives for an audience. An understanding of narrative is essential for students of the media because every text has a narrative.

> 'Whoever tells the stories of a culture has defined the terms, the agenda and the common issues we face.'
> George Gerbner, American academic

5 TELESCAPES: POPULAR TELEVISION

> 'These days, a television channel is just another product on an increasingly overcrowded television supermarket shelf. It is a brand.'
>
> Martin Lambie-Nairn

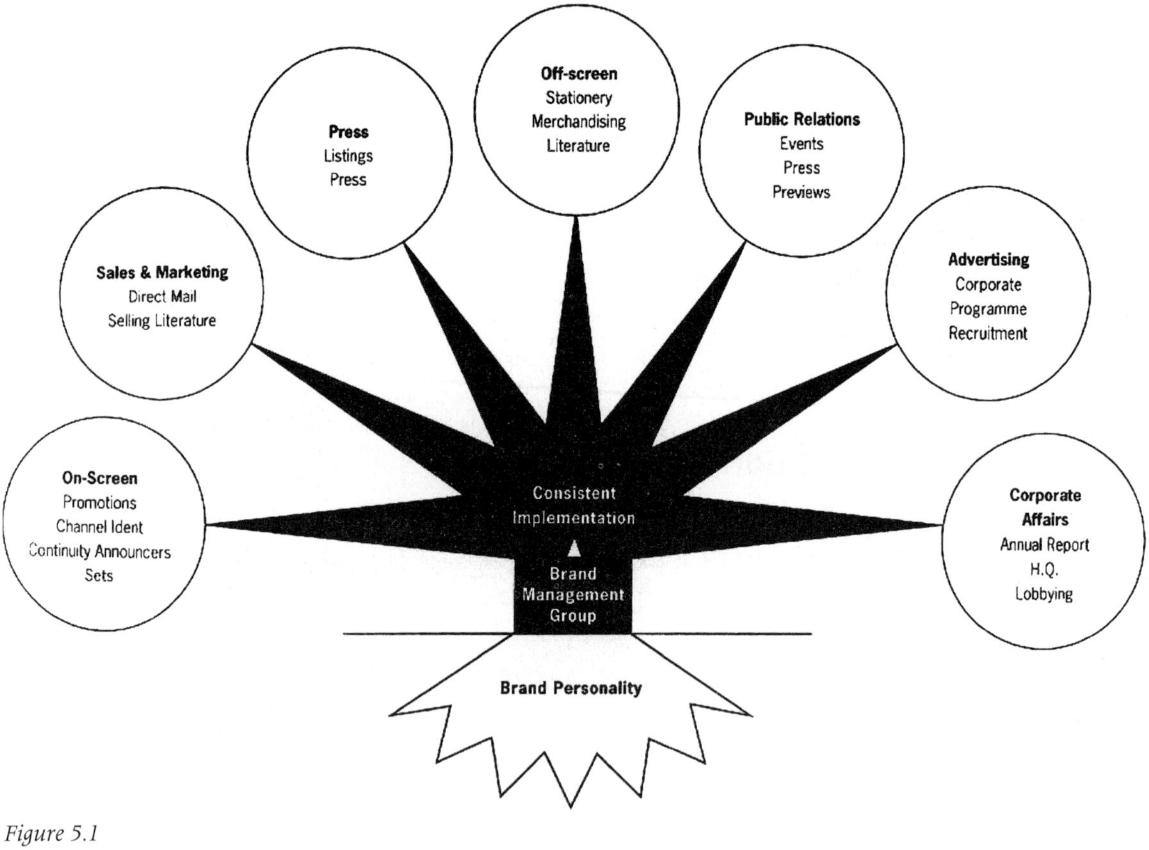

Press
Listings
Press

Off-screen
Stationery
Merchandising
Literature

Public Relations
Events
Press
Previews

Sales & Marketing
Direct Mail
Selling Literature

Advertising
Corporate
Programme
Recruitment

On-Screen
Promotions
Channel Ident
Continuity Announcers
Sets

Consistent
Implementation

Brand
Management
Group

Corporate Affairs
Annual Report
H.Q.
Lobbying

Brand Personality

Figure 5.1

Nature and purpose of television

- Primarily a domestic medium based on analogue technology and more recently digital technology. However, it has been used extensively by pubs in Great Britain, especially for screening sporting occasions.

- Access depends on the viewer's economic circumstances. Richer countries have more access to television sets in the home than poorer countries. Even in poorer countries television is important though it is more likely to be a communal experience.
- Billions of people watch great global occasions like the football World Cup.
- In Great Britain it is an important part of our daily lives.

Activity

Television and everyday life.

Look at Figure 5.2.

Use it to stimulate discussion of key moments in your class's experience of television.

EastEnders
(BBC1)

Frequency: 3 times weekly

Launched: 1985

Viewers: 12-18m depending on storyline

Defining moment:
On Christmas Day 1986, watched by an audience approaching 30m, "Dirty" Den Watts handed his wife Angie divorce papers, citing the fact she had feigned cancer. He was having an affair himself of course, and his adopted daughter Sharon's best friend Michelle Fowler was soon to become pregnant by him.
He was dead a year later, shot by a hitman on the banks of the canal

Brookside
(Channel 4)

Frequency: 3 times weekly

Launched: 1982

Audience: 3-4m

Defining moment:
The Jordache saga in 1995. In a plotline unprecedented in British soap history, abusive husband Trevor Jordache was murdered, then buried under the patio by his wife Mandy and daughter Beth (Anna Friel). Beth, who had previously featured in the first soap opera lesbian kiss, died in prison. Nine million tuned in waiting for Trevor to be exhumed, and to watch the subsequent murder trial

Coronation Street
(ITV)

Frequency: 4 times a week

Launched: 1960

Viewers: 12-18m

Defining moment:
The imprisonment of Deirdre Rachid (formerly Barlow) for credit card fraud. Duped by her conman boyfriend, Deirdre went down while he got away with a suspended sentence. As a "Free the Weatherfield One" campaign gathered strength, even the prime minister, Tony Blair, called for her release

Emmerdale
(ITV)

Frequency: 3-5 times a week

Launched: 1972

Viewers: 10-12m

Defining moment:
After years of rural calm interrupted by nothing more dramatic than raised voices at the Woolpack, the arrival of soap guru Phil Redmond (Grange Hill, Brookside) brought carnage to the Dales.
A plane crash saw off half the soap's established characters, with lesbian plotlines and downshifting yuppies following close behind

Figure 5.2

Tips

- Record your discussions. What was shared and what was personal?
- Are you all able to tell the story or do you have different versions?
- Make a list of great television moments. Give the list a title and illustrate it with pictures downloaded from the Internet
- Put appropriate quotes from your class into large speech bubbles and present as a class poster.

Activity   Repeated formats.

Extra information

- A series format is the most common format for television. A series format is a group of programmes which are linked thematically. The content of a production could be varied endlessly but the format could be repeated from programme to programme.
- Formats can be adapted, borrowed or sold.
- Formats appear right through television output. News, soaps and sitcoms are obvious examples.
- The need to get news reporters in the right place at the right time, for instance, leads to pressures of timing but it also creates further pressures because of limited budgets and quick turnover times.
- In drama programmes the necessity of producing episodes on a regular basis creates the need to have less rehearsal time and fewer 'takes'. Actors need to be employed on more than a one-off basis.

Task

Look at Figure 5.3.

Answer the following questions:

1. Explain the terms
   - 'broadcast networks' (paragraph 1);
   - 'bottom line' (paragraph 5);
   - 'narrowcasting' and 'niche programming' (paragraph 7);
   - 'rights' (paragraph 16).
2. Kevin Brockman is a spokesman of ABC (a Disney-owned network). Why does he call the show 'dramatic television'?
3. Explain what you understand of the 'format' of the British version of 'Who Wants to Be a Millionaire?'.

Who doesn't want to be a millionaire?

Edward Helmore on how an upstart import in rivalling ER in the US rating

FOR THE PAST three weeks, American television has been rocked by a nightly event that has caused the broadcast networks to rethink their entire programming strategy. It has also given social commentators an ideal vehicle upon which to hitch editorials about millennial madness and a country drunk on a booming economy.

The programme, an ABC-produced facsimile of the British game show *Who Wants to Be a Millionaire?*, has so dominated television that competitors have taken to writing off November – an all-important month for establishing advertising rates for the next quarter – as a complete aberration.

Over 18 consecutive nights this month, *Millionaire* – ABC paid UK producer Celador about $12 million for rights – has achieved the same ratings as the last Olympic Games in Nagano, Japan, the rights for which cost CBS $375m.

Broadcast in an 8.30pm slot usually reserved for expensive dramas and sitcoms, *Millionaire* has so crushed the competition that it now rivals the highest-rated show on TV, *ER*, with 29 million viewers. *Millionaire* pushed ABC's share of the audience up more than 30 per cent over the same month last year.

ABC president of sales Marvin Goldsmith said: 'It is going to help the network's bottom line tremendously.'

Though the network will not reveal official prices for commercial time during the show, it is understood that a 30-second slot costs between $300,000 and $500,000, rising to as much as $600,000 for advertisers wishing to buy in at the last moment. A slot during *ER* costs $545,000.

Millionaire's numbers surprised everybody when it was introduced in June as a summer filler. In a time of 'narrowcasting', when almost all programming is aimed at specific age groups, the show is a rare revival of the kind of mass-audience hit that the network works manufactured regularly before the advent of cable TV and niche programming.

'*Millionaire* has reiterated the power of broadcast television,' says ABC spokesman Kevin Brockman. 'It has shown that you can deliver a broad audience – young people and old, children and their parents.'

There are many theories about the programme's phenomenal success. As a genre, the game show was largely killed off at the peak of its popularity in the Fifties, after a succession of scandals involving rigged questions and false champions disillusioned the nation.

The time had come, says Michael Dann, former chief programmer at CBS, for the game show to rise again. 'There's a new generation that really doesn't care about the history of the game show,' he says. 'They just want good entertainment.'

ABC bought the show after its young British producer, Michael Davies, gave a copy to Stu Bloomberg, chairman of ABC Entertainment. 'We had never seen a game show like this,' he said. 'The music, the lighting, the whole gestalt of it was perfect.'

The fact that *Millionaire* was pulling in a 73 per cent share of the UK TV audience was also compelling. 'When you hear the words 73 per cent share, your ears do perk up,' he added.

But the show has done more than just revive the fortunes of the game show – and those of ABC, the Disney-owned network that routinely sits behind NBC and CBS in the ratings. Its astonishing impact has revealed something about America at a time of prosperity not seen since the Fifties. *New York Times* columnist Frank Rich called it 'the giddiest manifestations yet of a culture that offers a pornography of wealth almost everywhere you look'.

Almost everyone agrees that it bathes America in its favourite light – a feel-good show that reinforces the ideal of tolerance and opportunity. Says Brockman: 'You have people who, in the span of two days, go from a telephone call to changing their lives. It's the essence of dramatic television, and that's why it's so compelling.'

The other networks, which have seen dramas costing 10 times as much to produce get buried by a UK import with cheap production values, flashing disco lights and pulsing music, have taken notice.

NBC has bought the rights to *Master-mind* and Fox recently launched the bluntly titled *Greed*, an evil twin to *Millionaire* that was rushed into production in less than month.

Featuring teams of players rather than individual contestants, *Greed* boasts a jackpot of $2.25m and a predictable mantra: 'Do you feel the need for greed?'

'As you'd expect, the Fox show is aggressively sleazy,' wrote *Washington Post* TV critic Tony Kornheiser. 'Whereas Regis [Philbin, the host of *Millionaire*] warmly holds out a check for contestants to examine, [Chuck] Woolery whips out a gob of cash and commands: "Smell it! Smell the money".'

Not that Kornheiser was much kinder to *Millionaire*. In a critique last week titled 'Who wants to be an idiot?', he wrote: '*Millionaire* is a quiz show for people ugly enough to put out a fire just by showing up. You rarely see people like this on network TV – unless it's on *America's Most Wanted*.'

With the rush now on to duplicate ABC's success, NBC and CBS have decided to resurrect the games that were at the centre of the scandals of the Fifties: *21* and *The $64,000 Question*. ABC, meanwhile, is planning to bring the show back on a regular basis starting in January, probably at least twice and more likely three times a week.

For the time being, however, the network professes no concern at the impending stampede. 'Everyone in this company is just incredibly thrilled with the success of *Millionaire*,' says Brockman.

'And, as they say, imitation is the sincerest form of television.'

Figure 5.3

Tips

- Mise-en-scène.
- Presenters and contestants.
- Scheduling.

Extra information

- One simple way of interpreting the word 'popular' is to say that a programme is watched by a lot of people. By definition, media producers have to be able to attract an audience and the larger the audience, the more successful they are. Whether you hold a job in the media depends on the ability of the programme-makers to create the 'right' kind of media products for the audience.
- Media organisations have to compete for the audience. In the UK market we know that the television audience is fairly static but that the number of media organisations and the kinds of programmes which they transmit are growing.
- It is also clear that television organisations have to compete with other media such as film, video, surfing the Net and, more recently, computer games which were the big stocking filler for Christmas 1998.

Activity Audience ratings.

> 'The phenomenon of audience ratings has a very particular effect on television. It appears in the pressure to get things out in a hurry.'
> Pierre Bourdieu

Extra information

- What all media producers would give an arm and leg for is the formula that creates larger (better still, mass) audiences for their products. It is obvious that some formulas attract larger audiences than others. You could work that out by speaking to your friends and their friends, etc. about the best actors, pop stars, television personalities and quiz shows, just as you could find the best place for burgers or the best nightclub or whatever.
- What media producers also need to know is **how many** people are watching their programmes and **who** and **what kind of people** they are.
- These come about as the result of polling a representative sample whose viewing habits are used to represent the whole viewing population. Media organisations use other kinds of business organisations to collect these data on a regular basis.
- One organisation which collects these figures in the UK is called BARB

(Broadcasters' Audience Research Board). Approximately 4,500 households have meters attached to their television sets which record minute by minute the channel(s) being watched. It is owned jointly by the BBC and the ITCA (Independent Television Companies Association). The meter is fitted behind the television set and is operated by a hand-held remote control which has a button for each member of the household. The viewers punch their individual button to indicate that they are present in the room. The information is stored and sent to a central computer for analysis and presentation.

Task 1

List some disadvantages of such a system:

1.
2.
3.
4.

Extra information

⚫ The viewing day is divided into time slots: early morning, early afternoon, late afternoon, prime time (7pm to 10pm), late night and night-time,

⚫ Material has to be produced for most of these slots by major television organisations.

⚫ Television needs to produce 'fast thinkers' who can turn out programmes quickly.

⚫ This leads to conventionalised ways of doing things and 'low' production values.

⚫ It also leads to the use of imported formats which are cheap to buy.

Task 2: Researching time slots

Stage 1
Study any television viewing guide. (Each group should take a different television organisation.) Listings are very important and the organisations which have gone digital produce on-line guides.

Stage 2
Identify the major time slots and list the programmes falling within them.

Stage 3
Using a pie chart, categorise the programmes as:

⚫ entertainment, information or a combination
⚫ imported programmes.

Stage 4
Discuss what you learn about the audiences from the programme descriptions in each time slot.

Extra information

- The significance of 'attention grabbing' is significantly related to the race for the audience. Television makes a lot out of the numbers of people it attracts to its output.
- Sensationalism attracts attention.
- Television also calls for dramatisation of events (by the creation of conflict) and therefore exaggerates.
- It can and does draw attention to events – real or fictional – but in the process foregrounds the spectacular/spectacle.

Activity Scheduling.

Working definition

'. . . the organisation of television programmes over a week, so as to maximise their appeal to an audience. The process requires care because all channels are in competition with each other. A balance must be struck between keeping popular programmes in an established time-slot, and placing special material like "premiered" films at peak viewing times. Weaker programmes are often placed between two popular items in the hope that the audience will watch all three programmes.'

Stuart Price

Task 1

Study the following newspaper and magazine headlines about the BBC and ITV which appeared in 1999:

- THE RATINGS WARZONE;
- TEATIME BATTLE FOR 'NEWS AT TEN';
- THE FIGHT FOR EVENING SCHEDULE SUPREMACY;
- GEARING UP TO FIGHT ITV FOR LATE EVENING VIEWERS.

How is the idea of competition created?

Task 2

Extra information

> 'Weekend evenings, Saturday nights in particular, have been seen as the benchmark of the scheduler's audience-pulling skills – probably since ratings began. Saturdays have traditionally been evenings when the family was at home, with the inclination to slouch on the couch in front of the telly'.
>
> Peter Fiddick, journalist

1. How true a representation of your TV habits is this?
2. Compare BBC1 and ITV on a Saturday peak time viewing period by using a listings magazine or newspaper listings page.
3. How have the schedulers tried to attract and keep the audiences' attention?

Activity **Pulling the audience.**

Extra information

- The 1990s have seen the extensive and increasing use of trailers on all channels, increasing attention to programme idents and an increasing willingness to experiment with opening sequences.

- There has been an increase in the various ways in which television organisations promote themselves and their products.

- Television genre is one of the ways in which the audience recognises that a television programme is something that it wants to view. Television producers have only a few seconds (a fraction of a second?) before you 'zap'. As such, a programme must have recognisably familiar elements which attract or 'pull' you to the programme instantly to make you watch this rather than that. So they use a lot of 'short cuts' like recognisable locations, characters (real or imaginary), and recognisable ways of addressing the audience.

- A key feature of scheduling is that media producers want to repeat things which have worked for audiences before at a familiar time. Media producers and audiences like the familiar; just look at what controversies are caused by the moving of favourite programmes to different time slots or when media presenters change to a different channel.

- The key is viewer familiarity with timing, formats, characters and plots. The audience has certain kinds of expectations to draw on which may come from a variety sources.

- The activity of watching a lot of television, for instance, is a key and this draws attention to the fact that television has a whole set of histories of viewing on which to draw.
- We do not all share the same history of viewing television and recent technological developments mean that the audience is becoming increasingly fragmented
- However, media producers also have to 'refresh' formats, characters and plots otherwise they become stale and predictable.

Some conventional formats for television and films on television

The Picaresque Hero/Heroine
This kind of media drama production recounts the adventures of a likeable character who tends to get into all kinds of scrapes. It usually has a simple plot and is episodic in structure, consisting of a series of adventures happening to the hero (heroine) whose character changes little. Often the hero has henchmen or women to help him or her. Its tone is likely to be somewhat amoral (frequent love affairs) and satirical (poking fun at contemporary issues).

Examples: 'Moll Flanders', 'Vanity Fair', 'Emma', 'Tom Jones' and 'Sharpe'.

Task 1
Does Bond (1960 onwards) fall into this format or Frost (ITV, 1997 onwards)?

They are often based on books and are adapted for television or film. It is a common feature of situation comedies.

Task 2

Stage 1
Research 'Hancock's Half Hour' or 'Some Mothers Do 'Ave 'Em' or 'One Foot in the Grave'. Use the Internet as a resource.

Stage 2
Produce a 'factfile' for a listings magazine which will give the modern reader the necessary background to the series and attract them to a special showing of a single episode on UK Gold.

Boy Meets Girl

Task 3
Study the Bollywood poster in Figure 5.4. Make a list of the conventional features of Bollywood movies.

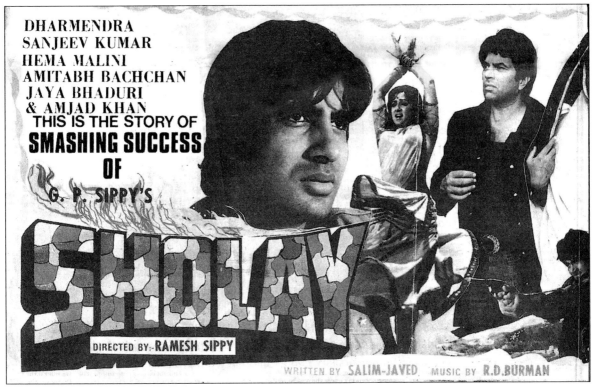

Figure 5.4

The Buddies

- Traditionally, buddy films are for the boys. The narrative centres on the friendship between two male characters.
- The genre was much in vogue in the 1960s and 1970s ('Butch Cassidy and the Sundance Kid'). The friendship is invariably heterosexual since the heroes are always doing action-packed things together.
- It expanded in the 1980s and 1990s to include proto-father–son relationship (as in 'Colour of Money' with Paul Newman and Tom Cruise or 'Indiana Jones and the Last Crusade' with Sean Connery and Harrison Ford).
- The maleness of the genre has also been called into question in films like 'Thelma and Louise' which has two female buddies (parodied in the Peugeot advertisement).
- With the advent of AIDS, the genre has also started to include films which involve male gay friendship.
- Television and radio have an enormously long tradition of comedy pairings.
- It is also a format used on news and lifestyle programmes, often in

Tips

Stage 1: What's their history?
Male/female? Age? Personality? Tastes? Skills? Experiences? Beliefs?
Interests?

Give them a provisional name.

Stage 2: Relationships

Strong? Confident? Outgoing? Loner? Fashion conscious? Scatty? Do they upset
other people?

Stage 3: How do they speak?
Insider? Figure of fun? Speech impediment? Characteristic way of speaking?
Dialect?

Stage 4: What do they look like?
Familiar? Ordinary? Stereotypical?

Stage 5: How do they react? First impressions
In an argument? Are they manipulative? Open? Honest? Are they a victim or a
'go-getter' and problem-solver?

Plan some 'walk throughs' of when they first meet other characters in the soap.

(Definition: A walk through is when you produce a short piece of script, give it
to the characters and let them act it out.)

Stage 6: Researching actors to play the part
- Make suggestions for some well-known people from the British media who
  could be the kind of 'actor' you have in mind.
- Look for faces in the magazines for people with the 'typical' look of your
  character.
- If you need to, produce an 'identikit' of your character.

Task 4: An A–Z of issues

Extra information
- Controversy is never far from television drama.
- To attract new viewers it constantly seeks to cross boundaries and
  explore issues through the issues which the characters have to face.
- Sensationalism is often a key 'drama value'.

Make an alphabetical list of issues in television drama.

Tips
- You will need to share ideas on this and build up the list as you go.

- A TV listings magazine will be helpful.
- Examples to start you off:

A : animal rights, abuse (child/solvent)
L: lottery success, lottery addiction
S: stabbing, stalking
V: video surveillance, video (home)
Z: zoos (escape from)

Task 5: Grabbing the headlines

Extra information

- There is an enormous amount of discussion in all media about other media programmes as well as in our daily lives.
- Talk shows, newspapers, magazines, news items and discussions/chats/ gossip in our personal lives all add to our sense of what is at stake in terms of the representation of events in television drama.

Study the following headlines and opening paragraphs from various newspapers when 'Brookside' (Channel 4) screened a controversial kiss in August 1996:

1. *Daily Mail*
   'STORM OVER TV INCEST SCENE'
   'A scene depicting incest plunged Channel 4 into a new storm over indecency last night.'
2. *Daily Mirror*
   'FURY OVER TV INCEST'
   'Brookside bosses were slammed last night for screening an incest scene.'
3. *Liverpool Echo*
   'TV SEX SCENE SPARKS FURY'
   'Brookside makers remained defiant today after an incest scene was shown last night.'
4. *Teesside Evening Gazette*
   'CRITICS SLAM "SCURRILOUS" INCEST SCENE'
   'TV Soap Brookside has been condemned for showing a brother and sister lying in bed after having sex.'
5. *Yorkshire Post*
   '"UNFORGIVABLE" BROOKSIDE BREAKS THE LAST TABOO'
   'TV soap Brookside was condemned last night for showing a brother and sister lying in bed after sex.'
6. *Daily Record*
   'BROOKIE'S NOOKIE IS BIG DRAW'

Tips

- characters;
- locations;
- objects;
- typical narratives – 'means ... motive ... opportunity', 'bodies', 'cliff hangers', 'victims', 'procedures'.

Stage 2

Brainstorm the sorts of features which might be different.

Tips

- locations;
- gender;
- violence;
- style of presentation;
- viewpoint.

Task 3: Character types

- Make a collection of the characters who appear in your sample.
- Classify them in some way: 'good cop/bad cop', 'young female inspector/old male inspector'.
- Design a poster or an A4 page to illustrate the classifications.

Tips

- Listing magazines are good for this.
- If you can, use an editing programme like Microsoft Publisher.
- Give your poster a title ('Great TV Cops', 'Gotcha!').
- Use magazines or download from the Web to get your images.
- Write some captions to anchor the images.
- Use an exciting font (trace from magazines if in trouble here).

Task 4: Narrative themes

Extra information

- The fraternity: this emphasises teamwork and partnership. Not rocking the boat. Supporting colleagues. Conflict arises out of roles and behaviour under pressure from the job, colleagues, partners and superiors. Secret affairs are a common motif.
- The individual: this focuses on a single viewpoint. Conflict comes about through relationships with superiors and colleagues (often inept or corrupt). Problems with authority and procedures are common. Persistence is a key attribute in the face of continuing criticism. The individual often has special skills or qualities which mark them out as the problem-solver. They can unlock the puzzle set by the narrative.

Stage 1
Plan a typical police team for a show to be set in your area.

Tips
- gender;
- age;
- ethnicity;
- insider/outsider;

Stage 2
Give them names.

Stage 3
Profile them.

Stage 4
Present your ideas to the group.

Tips
- What did they expect?
- What didn't they expect?
- What impressed them about your ideas?

Task 5: Narrative structures

Extra information
- Time is always compressed. A robbery or murder takes a lot longer than half an hour to solve!
- Flashbacks are frequently used. Visual reminders often. Hidden clues whose significance is not apparent on first viewing.
- Events can be in non-chronological order or made to appear simultaneous in order to enhance suspense or offer a variety of viewpoints on an event.
- Information may be withheld from the characters or from the audience for a variety of dramatic reasons.
- Clues of all kinds may mislead the police or the audience.
- Stories are often juxtaposed. As with soaps, there can be many stories running at the same time, each offering different viewpoints and each coming to resolutions which may be 'open' or 'closed'.
- Public roles and private relationships are often juxtaposed.

Study an example of an hour-long serial like 'The Bill'.

Stage 1
Identify the stories running in the episode.

Stage 2
With a stopwatch, time the length of the sequences devoted to each story.

Stage 3
Do the stories have the structure of 'open' or 'closed' narratives?

Stage 4
Are some stories more important than others?

Task 6: Visual conventions

Extra information
- Media producers of police and detective series have a range of constraints, not the least being the budget for the production.
- 'Lavish production values' depend on time, availability and money.
- 'Lavish production values' and 'the art of the possible' go hand-in-hand for media producers.
- The type, timing and potential ratings determine the production's 'values'.
- Innovative techniques and new approaches are rarer than typical methods of presentation. Critics often praise 'new' and 'innovative' techniques.

Study an example of a detective serial or series which has been much praised by television critics. Examples are 'Prime Suspect' and other work by Lynda La Plante.

For a single episode:

Stage 1
Study the use of camera angles. List the different kinds of shots used.

Stage 2
Study the use of frames and the construction of the mise-en-scène.

Stage 3
Study the techniques of editing: cross-cutting, rapidity of shots, continuity.

Stage 4
Study specific genre techniques: aerial shots, car chases, extreme close-ups, lighting.

Advanced task
What do you understand by the word 'quality' when applied to detective and police series?

Tips
- People argue that some are 'better' than others. Why and how?
- Do lavish production values make some productions better than others?

- Does hiring well-known 'stars' and 'personalities' to play the parts give 'quality'?
- Is it the story or the plot which gives the production 'quality'?

Advanced investigations: Television drama 3

Viewing television drama trailers.

Activity

Extra information
- Trailers must identify the product. The title is critical.
- Trailers can be familiar or challenging.
- Trailers must create expectations.
- Trailers must make 'promises' to deliver the expectations.
- Trailers must set up a 'need to see'.

Task

View a recent trailer. Watch it carefully on the first viewing. On the second viewing, complete Table 5.2.

Tips
- If each group makes notes on one element it will be easier.
- Combine your findings afterwards.

Title and organisation	
What does the title tell you about the production?	
What do you associate with the channel 'values' in terms of drama?	
What expectations do these elements create?	
Narrative	
Identify the main features of the drama	
Identify its genre	
Does the trailer have a 'narrative' structure?	
Characters	
Identify the main characters	
Are they familiar?	
Are there any surprises in the way they have been cast?	
Are there heroes and heroines or obvious villains?	
How is conflict created?	
Visual codes	
Number of shots?	
Type of shots?	
Lighting?	
Locations?	
Audio codes	
Music? Parallel? Contrapuntal?	
Voice-over	
Voices and the dialogue	
Audience	
Pre- or post-watershed?	
Controversial?	
Challenging?	
Enigmatic? Posing a question?	
Visual style?	
Typical format?	
Enjoyment	
Would you enjoy?	
Why?	
Why not?	

Table 5.2

Activity **Practical work: Storyboarding trailers.**

Information
- BBC 2 is planning a short season of 'repeats' of 'classic' television adaptations over a six-week period.
- Part of the strategy is to support the idea that the BBC needs to increase the licence fee so that it can go on producing 'high-quality versions' of classic novels.
- It will have a specified time slot on Sunday evenings between 6pm and 8pm.
- It will be called ' Serialzone'.

Tips
- Think carefully about the scheduling of the individual adaptations.
- Research 'classic' adaptations from the BBC website.
- Choose your favourites.
- Think carefully about the audience.

Task 1
Storyboard the trailer for this season.

Tips
- Include clips from at least three adaptations
- Include famous characters
- Include famous sayings
- Refer to key moments
- Flag up BBC2
- Use voice-over to give the key promises to the audience
- Add music
- Announce when and where

Do not exceed two minutes!

Task 2
Evaluate the storyboard of your trailer.

Tips
- Describe your approach to the task.
- Describe the key decisions the group made: arguments for and against particular approaches.
- Describe how you planned a narrative.
- Explain how you 'branded' the season as a BBC2 production.

Investigating television chat shows

Activity   Chat shows.

> 'I understand the push for ratings caused programmers to air what is popular, and that is not going to change. I am embarrassed by how far over the line the topics have gone, but I also recognise my contribution to this phenomenon.'
>
> Oprah Winfrey

Extra information

- Chat shows have always been an important feature of the television schedules. As a genre the various forms were used extensively (as many forms were) on the radio.
- They most often appear as part of the daytime schedule, though not exclusively.
- The most familiar form has a host, guests (sometimes a single guest) who are media personalities or stars, and a studio audience.
- The guests are interviewed (in a friendly and supportive manner, usually) by the host and provide stories, anecdotes and observations which amuse and entertain the watching audience both in the studio and in the country at large.
- The guests also promote their latest venture or announce a career change or build their status. They tend not to be too controversial.
- The 1990s have witnessed considerable changes, partly as the result of American imported programmes used to fill up the schedules quickly, and the need of media organisations to attract controversy using sensational means. The process has sometimes been called 'dumbing down'. Another term used is 'tabloidisation'.
- These newer-format chat shows have hosts who are well-known media personalities, guests from the 'real world' who are not normally seen on television (except perhaps docusoaps) and a 'participating' audience.

Task 1: The traditional chat show format

Extra information

- Presenters tend to be drawn from the world of news or current affairs: Michael Aspel, Michael Parkinson, Kilroy, Clive James, Clive Anderson and Brian Walden. They have journalistic, parliamentary or legal backgrounds.
- They are safe and authoritative.
- They offer common-sense and balanced views of issues.

- They control the interviews and only invite the views of the audience on their own terms.
- They are most often men although men/women partnerships have developed.

Stage 1
Choose some traditional hosts.

Stage 2
List some of the typical guests who appear with them.

Stage 3
Spider diagram the particular approach they bring to the host's job.

Tips
- Clive Anderson uses comedy and ridicule.
- Parkinson is often like a fan.

Task 2: Newer-format chat shows

Extra information
- As a media student you should be wary of anything claiming to be new or original!
- The hosts tend to come out of the 'entertainment industry': for example, in America Jerry Springer (1991), Ricki Lake (1995), in Great Britain Lily Savage, Dame Edna Everage, Ian Wright and Julian Clary. They are flamboyant, outrageous, opinionated and passionate. Often draw attention to issues of sexuality.
- The controlling host remains (Oprah, Jerry Springer, Vanessa, Trisha) but with a different function. Their job is to create sound bites of conflict, crisis and resolution.
- They become 'narrative entertainers' who bring the show to a triumphant and satisfying conclusion.
- The role of the audience has changed 'dramatically': it takes sides passionately, is encouraged to intervene through whoops and interventions and members make up their minds on the issue being discussed.
- The host delivers the 'judgement' at the end.
- The topics changed from issues of social concern to the general public to the behaviour of private citizens 'outing' their concerns on television. The new emphasis is on confession, personal testimony and recognition of what you are and whatever you do.
- Gender and relationships are definitely a part of the agenda.
- Conventional behaviour patterns are opened out for public approval or disapproval.

'Kilroy' (BBC 1, daytime)

This is a good show to study as it bridges the gap between the more 'information'-based programmes and 'entertainment' by dealing with a topical issue (often raised by the news industry) with an involved studio audience who are 'victims' or 'witnesses'. Most of the audience have stories to tell.

View a typical show and in groups make notes on **one** of the following topics:

- The topic and what you already knew about it from other sources.
- Kilroy's qualities as a host.
- The different viewpoints represented: how 'expert' were they? Were they based on personal experience?
- The way in which the issue was resolved.

Share your findings.

Task 3: Faking it: The guests

Extra information

- The genre has always been 'sensational' and has throughout its history caused controversy. Rod Hull and Emu, George Best and Oliver Reed on 'Parkinson', for instance. They have often dealt with controversial topics and used controversial 'stars' at the height of a scandal (Sharon Stone, Helen Mirren).
- The style has changed. They are more 'shows' than 'chats'. The emphasis is on guests 'acting out' parts which draw attention to the constructed nature of the event. The audience is part of the act. The question for the watching audience becomes not what kind of people are the guests but whether they are 'real'. This is part of the fascination for the watching audience.
- The controversy over 'fake' guests has been a part of the debate for over a decade and is not new. It arrived from America along with the newer formats.

Stage 1

Study the front page article of the Mirror (12 February 1999) Figure 5.7.

- List five typical features.
- Describe the pictures.
- Explain how they have been used.
- Explain the use of 'expose', 'scandal', 'fake', 'duped', 'sensational disclosure' as key tabloid 'values'.

WE EXPOSE ANOTHER TV SHOW SCANDAL

TRISHA IS FAKE TOO

Fatogram's 'lover' was a paid actor

EXCLUSIVE

ITV's flagship daytime show Trisha has also been duped by fake guests.

A rolypolygram girl's "lover" was an actor she only met the night before. A male model — who also admitted fooling Vanessa Feltz and The Time..The Place — and his former "girlfriend" were strangers.

The new scandal follows our sensational disclosure that guests fed Vanessa's rival BBC show with a string of lies. Two producers and a researcher have been suspended.

As shaken TV chiefs pledged tighter procedures, Trisha Goddard said last night: "We check everything. But the reality is one or two people are going to slip through the net."

Yesterday, Sharon Tolfers told how she posed as a buxom brunette on Trisha while out-of-work actor Noel Anthony

By MATTHEW WRIGHT and NIC NORTH

appeared as her boyfriend Graham. The 30-year-old single mum revealed that she was hired by the same man who took Vanessa for a ride — agency boss Tony Papotto.

Sharon said: "I got a call from Tony asking me if I wanted to go on the Trisha show. He said he wanted someone who was

TURN TO PAGE 2

DUPED: Trisha

DUPED: Vanessa

HOAXERS: Sharon and actor Noel pretended they were lovers — they only met the day before

Stop fighting over my fat!

'LOVERS' HAD NEVER MET BEFORE

FROM PAGE ONE
fat but keen to lose weight and a partner who wanted them to stay as they were.

"He said not to worry about the other person as he would fix someone up."

Sharon was contacted with travel arrangements for filming in Norwich. Meanwhile Noel got a call to ring Papotto.

The two "lovers" met at London's Liverpool Street station before travelling to

Norfolk. On the journey they discussed what story to tell. The next day they were filmed.

Sharon, of Walthamstow, East London, said: "I was astonished how easy it all was. I spoke to a few people on the show but they didn't carry out any checks.

"Even when they were filming I thought 'I can't believe we are getting away with this.' There Noel and I were rowing about whether

I should lose weight or not and I hardly knew the bloke!"

Noel, of Earls Court, West London, said: "Tony told me I was to play a bloke called Graham who didn't want his girlfriend to lose weight.

"One of the researchers rang me on my mobile but she only asked what I did for a living. I said I was a labourer which I'm not.

"Later, we had a briefing from the producers – they kept saying we had to

appear to be loving.

"They didn't ask questions to verify who we were. I got the impression they just wanted a good show." The couple put on such a good act that Sharon was cheered by the studio audience and Noel booed.

Male model Eddie Wheeler, 34, of South London, duped three shows. He told The Mirror: "The fact that people like me can appear on these shows and tell a

different story each time makes a mockery of daytime TV."

BBC director of Broadcasting Matthew Bannister said of the Vanessa fakes: "We are carrying out the most thorough investigation we possibly can.

"We are also putting in place a thorough review of research procedures on all programmes which involve members of the public."

● Voice of the Mirror – Page 6

Figure 5.7

Source: The Mirror, 12 February 1999

Stage 2
Study 'Voice of The Mirror' (12 February 1999) in Figure 5.8.

Discuss the following questions:

1. How do you know a film, play or a soap on TV' is not 'real'?
2. Do you feel that the Mirror has a point?
3. Do you still feel that these shows are 'factual' shows? Does it matter?

Bosses must take blame
for this shameful deceit

WHEN you watch a film, play or a soap on TV, you know it is not real.

But factual programmes are supposed to be what their name says – fact, not fiction.

Yesterday and again today The Mirror has revealed that some of those who appear in shows like Vanessa and Trisha are not what they pretend to be.

These are hardly the first television scandals.

There was the totally made-up documentary about drug-running. There was the film about rent boys who were not rent boys at all. There was the programme about a father and daughter who were actually boy and girlfriend.

Each of these was a hoax, or, to put it bluntly, a lie.

The top people involved with the channels and shows say they did not know what was happening. They claim they were hoaxed, too.

Obsessed

But they cannot be excused for what is going wrong with television in this country – and remember, they are the ones who boast that it is the best TV in the world.

They are always swift to attack the press for "dumbing down" or getting things wrong.

Yet they have become obsessed with the drive for good ratings – which means getting lots of viewers.

There are two points about that. One is the hypocrisy of people who pretend to be whiter than white while allowing their own standards to slip into the gutter. The other, more crucially, is the way viewers are allowed to be cheated.

If these factual programmes were presented as make-believe shows, there would be little wrong with them.

What is outrageous is that fiction is presented as fact. And some of the most senior people in television must share the blame because THEY insist on ever-more sensational shows.

In the past year we have witnessed documentaries showing someone dying, nudity, the lives of transvestite prostitutes and sexual fetishists.

The Mirror does not object to difficult and controversial subjects being dealt with in drama. But when factual television is concerned with nothing but sensation and thrill-seeking, disaster is bound to follow. The response to The Mirror's Vanessa revelations was sadly predictable.

Vanessa went on air to express her horror and apologise. Two producers and a researcher have been sent home – which means they will probably be fired. But there will be plenty of people desperate to get on in television who will be ready to take their place. And to commit the same wrongs.

Nothing will change until the culture

that has invaded factual programming is abandoned.

And remember, we are not just talking here about commercial TV but about the BBC, too – the proud upholder of public-service television which still boasts of its impeccable standards.

The bosses should not commission shows which put makers under such pressure that they are tempted to cheat.

Preaching

If actors are to be used instead of real people, then tell us. It will still be entertaining.

What we want to stop is the TV companies allowing lies to be told to viewers while preaching to the press.

The obvious way to show they want to clean up television is to make the people at the top take responsibility.

If a few heads rolled, things would change fast.

Newspapers are accused of many evils and we sometimes get things wrong. But it is rare for a paper to lie. Certainly The Mirror never would.

Factual television needs to adopt those standards. To respect truth and present facts and people as they are.

If it does not, there will be only one possible result. Viewers will switch off in ever greater numbers.

Figure 5.8   *Source: Voice of the Mirror*

4. Do you feel that the *Mirror* is more concerned to tell a good media story than really attacking the broadcast media? After all, the basis of good tabloid journalism is a simple conflict!

Task 4: Questions of regulation: ITC

Study 'The Programme Complaints and Interventions Report' (January 1996) (Figure 5.9).

Discuss the following questions:

● What are the expectations of daytime television?
● Do you feel that Anglia ITV was 'crossing the line' with this show?

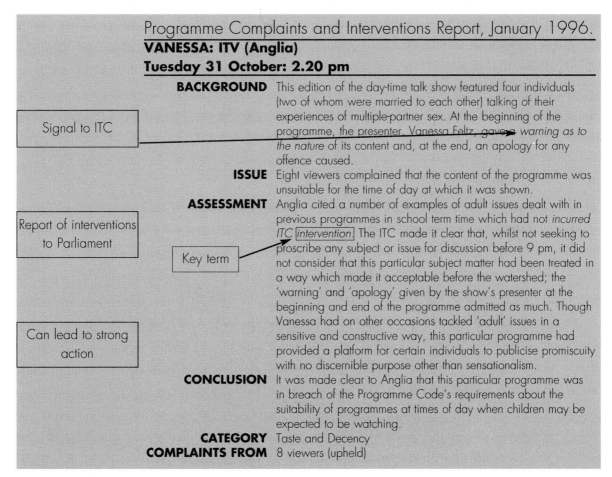

Figure 5.9

Task 5: Your own chat show

Extra information
- Many of the newer chat shows are deliberately provocative and challenge the boundaries of what is acceptable. They can be very 'in your face'.
- Regulation of what you produce will come from inside your school or institution if you choose a newer-style show. You will not be able to assume that your approach will be acceptable.

Tips
- Use evaluation to explore the issues raised. What was allowed and what wasn't in your school?
- Evaluate every stage of the production process.

Stage 1
Decide on the 'style'.

Stage 2
Profile your host.

Tip
You may invent a new personality.

Stage 3
Design the set.

Tip
If the audience is a key component of the show, how will you seat them in order to show them off?

Stage 4
Plan camera positions and types of camera movements.

Stage 5
Research guests.

Tips
- They may not be 'real'.
- You may need a script for them.
- You may need to profile them.
- You may need to rehearse them.

Stage 6
How will you plan the 'encounters' with the host: as a typical narrative of initial situation, conflict/trial/test, resolution?

Tip

Many shows use contrasting pairs to create conflict.

Stage 7: Production sheet

Use a production sheet to help you.

Tips

- Plan a title sequence and time it.
- Break into timed segments (six is typical, with commercial breaks).

Stage 8

Plan how and where you wish the audience to intervene. Plan the type of interventions (boo, hiss, applaud, whoop, sigh, cheer).

Stage 9

Shoot.

Tip

Remember to evaluate each stage.

6 FILMSCAPES: READING AND SELLING FILM

Information

- We are sophisticated readers of film even though most of the time we are not aware that we are 'reading'.
- This is because we have become so used to the language of films that we automatically read signs. For example, if we see a shot of a lonely house, with a full moon, the sound of owls hooting and wind in the trees, we will expect to be viewing a horror film.
- Similarly, the signs of horses, tumbleweed and stetsons alert us to the Western genre. **Generic codes** help us make meaning and arouse our expectations. Such signs rely on our foreknowledge or, in other words, our **past experiences** of film watching.
- Our ability to 'read' audiovisual images is even more complicated than recognising past signs as film has a language of its own the foundations of which were cemented in the Silent period (1900–29).
- These were honed to the conventions we have come to expect during the Hollywood Studio period (1930–50).

Activity   **Self-test.**

Task 1
In order to see how films make meaning, give explanations of the following questions:

- How do we know that a story is going into the past?
- How can we tell where the action is taking place?
- How can we tell that events are happening simultaneously?
- How can we tell how a character is feeling inside?
- How can we tell that someone in close-up is actually speaking to someone else?

Tip
These are some of the questions early film-makers set themselves in trying to create narratives.

Task 2

Extra information

- The Hollywood Studio system began in the Silent period but was at its height from 1930–50 although it continues to dominate world cinema even today.
- In its heyday the big film companies such as MGM, Fox and Warner Brothers controlled distribution as well as making films. Stars, directors, script writers and even manual workers were under contract to the studio which meant that they had little control over projects and made the films the studios wanted. Although it is often stated that the studios controlled output and restricted experimentation, many great films were made in the period and some artists managed to work well within the restrictions.
- Hollywood recruited some of the best directors, cinematographers and script writers from Europe and America. The studios were very powerful but many artists enjoyed the security they provided while for others they were places of conflict as artists tried to choose their own projects.

Compare your thoughts on the questions given with the information in Table 6.1.

Investigating narrative

Extra information

- Most films tell a story but it is **how** they tell stories which is interesting.
- Some critics have argued that there are only three structures for stories: the mystery, the search and the journey.

Activity   **Typical film structures.**

Task 1

Stage 1
Try thinking of five films and see if they will fit those strußctures.

Stage 2
Choose two films and spend time jotting down the following:

- Briefly what happens.
- Type of plot. Genre.
- List the main characters.

The past
There are several ways in which film-makers answered this. One way was to use **fade-out** behind the characters, or for the screen to go misty or for a narrator to signal the past with commentary.

Can you think of any films where such techniques are used?

The setting
In Hollywood films it was a convention that before we saw characters, we had a shot of the building they were in. This is called an **establishment shot** as it establishes where the action is taking place. Hollywood producers were concerned that audiences should always understand what was happening so that if a film moved about a great deal then the place and/or time would go up on the screen and maps would be used to show journeys.

Can you think of examples of any of these techniques in films you have seen?

Simultaneous action
Unless the screen is split so that we can see more than one action, time has to be tampered with and extended in the cinema. If in a silent film we see a girl tied to a railway track, followed by the train approaching, followed by a rescue party on its way, we realise that all of these are happening simultaneously. It is a key way in which film-makers create suspense and excitement.

Can you think of an action movie where time is extended in this way so that we can see what is happening to all the main characters?

Character feelings
The close-up is an important shot in cinema because it takes us into the mind of the character so that we can see the slightest nuance in the face. Film-makers quickly saw how visual signs could help to indicate the mood of a character. There are many elements which contribute to our impression of a character, including *mise-en-scène*, particularly make-up, costume, setting and music.

Look at a favourite character of yours and make a list of the things which contribute to the character's impact.

Interaction between characters
In the early days of silent cinema if two characters were in a scene then they would be shown together for the whole of the scene as cameras were heavy and static and it was the actors who moved in and out of frame. As cameras became more developed and film language became more sophisticated, film-makers created a technique of filming dialogue which has become an accepted way of filming. They would usually begin with an establishment shot to show that there were two people in the room, then move to a close-up, reverse the shot and so on.

One of the things they had to be careful of was **eyeline matching**, for if the actor in close-up was not looking at the exact spot where the other protagonist was situated then the film looked disjointed or even comic. The smoothness of such filming creates conventions we expect in films.

Our expectations can be played with by film-makers. In 'Forever Young' there is no establishment shot. Mel Gibson speaks to the girl he loves and then the camera pulls back to show us that he is talking to an empty seat. This is the reason why the first shot was dispensed with.

As you look at films, try to notice how film-makers deal with dialogue scenes.

Table 6.1

Task 2: Narrative (again)

The narrative theorist Tzvetan Todorov says that narrative is created through three stages:

1. A state of **equilibrium**. A sort of calm before anything happens.
2. The **disruption** of this equilibrium by an event.
3. The successful **restoration** of equilibrium through action.

Look at the films you have chosen and see how this structure fits your narrative. How is it done?

Write notes to show that you can apply the theory.

Task 3

Extra information
Vladimir Propp, a Russian critic, has analysed plots in terms of folk tales and shown a pattern of stock characters who appear in stories. His ideas have been adapted by others and typical characters might include:

- the hero, who is the main character, on some kind of quest;
- the villain who will stand in the way of the hero;
- the mentor or teacher who will provide guidance;
- the helper who will aid the hero in some way;
- the princess who acts as a reward for the hero and will be threatened by the villain;
- her father who will reward the hero for his quest;
- the donor who will provide help through a gift.

Although in older tales the gender of the characters is obvious, in the twenty-first century we are likely to see more role-reversals, with women as heroes and men as princesses. Some films which are close to folk tales, such as 'The Phantom Menace' (1999), can easily have characters put into such categories.

Stage 1
Try doing this with the films you have made notes on.

Stage 2
Create profiles for three of the character types above for a new film in a particular genre.

Investigating identification

Extra information

- When we are watching a film we are only given the information that the director chooses to give us. The viewpoint we are given is not always clear.

- We tend to identify with the hero. That identification can be built up by the presence of a star we admire, through camera angles so that we are positioned with the hero and by the information which we are given. For example, sometimes we know the same information as the hero and sometimes we know more so that we can fear for the hero and care about him so that we are drawn into the story and become involved.

- In the film 'Lady in the Lake' (1946), identification was taken to extremes as in this detective story we only see the hero when he looks in the mirror. Thus the heroine kisses the camera and the villain punches it. This is an attempt to put us in the place of the hero.

- Something similar occurs at the beginning of 'Dark Passage' (1947) where Humphrey Bogart escapes from prison and we see things through his eyes until he has an operation to change his appearance.

- Other techniques used by film-makers include voice-over which lulls us into thinking we are seeing the truth when we are actually seeing only a version. Voice-over always implies a partial point of view.

- Sometimes, as in 'Braveheart' (1995), we are surprised because it is not until the very end of the film that the identity of the narrator is revealed (in this case, as Robert the Bruce).

- Most films are made up of partly **omniscient narration**, where we know more than the hero and follow more than one character, and some **restricted narration**, where we know exactly the same as the protagonist.

- In *film noir* films such as 'Double Indemnity' (1944) or films like 'Bladerunner' (1982) which owe a great deal to that genre, we tend to see things through the hero's eyes as we are governed by voice-over. We rarely see things which the hero does not see (except where tension is created by showing us in advance what the hero is to face) and heroines are particularly mysterious as we see them through the hero's mind.

- Some films play with such versions by giving us different versions of the truth. An early film to do this was 'Crossfire' (1947) where the murder of a Jew is investigated and the evidence of several soldiers shown to us as versions of the truth.

- A modern film which uses the same technique is 'Courage under Fire' (1996) where Denzel Washington is investigating how Meg Ryan, an officer in the Gulf War, died, and we are given different versions of the story by different soldiers.

This playing with narrative allows us to choose which version we identify with. Identification with characters is an important element of film narrative.

Working definitions

Omniscient narrative

This style of filming gives the audience the impression that it is seeing everything and is in a better position to follow what is happening than the hero. Sometimes the audience will find out things that the hero does not know, so that it can anticipate what is going to happen.

Restricted narrative

The audience is put in the same situation as the hero and knows what the hero knows. Things that are a mystery for the hero remain so for the audience as well. A good example is a detective film where the camera follows the detective uncovering the clues and until the end, when all is revealed, the audience is equally mystified.

Film noir

Argument has existed as to whether this is a genre or a style. The style of odd angles, sharp contrasts of lighting and framing of objects helps define the genre. *Film noir* films are characterised by use of voice-over, restless heroes, blonde scheming heroines and a world of crime, particularly murder. 'Double Indemnity' (1944) is usually cited as the mother of the genre.

Activity   Film study.

Task 1: Aspects of a film

Stage 1
Look at the film 'North by North West' (1959), directed by Alfred Hitchcock.

Stage 2
As you watch, groups should make notes on different aspects: identification, use of dialogue, establishment shots and feelings of characters. Share your findings.

Task 2: Planning a treatment
Read this 'urban myth':

A man reverses his car into an empty, stationary vehicle. There are quite a few people standing around watching him. He gets out of his car with a pen and paper, writes something and places it on the windscreen of the damaged vehicle.

129

Camera language

A *shot* describes a single recording. A number of shots combine to make a *sequence*. A successful sequence will be made up of a number of different shots, which serve different functions, but which are all a means of conveying the overall action of the sequence in an entertaining and stimulating way for the viewer.

SHOT SIZES

Most shots are usually described in terms of the human figure. These are standard points of reference in any kind of film or video work. A knowledge of this terminology enables all those involved in the production processes to have a common understanding of what is required for each shot, from initial storyboard to final production stages.

▲ When you edit from one shot to another, it is important that there is a decisive difference of shot size or angle from one to the other.

MEDIUM CLOSE UP (MCU)

From above the top of the head to just below the shoulders, this shot shows significant details of one individual. The background has become secondary to the main interest of the composition.

CLOSE UP (CU)

Top of the head to just below the chin

BIG CLOSE-UP (BCU)

This intrusive shot, from forehead to chin, has dispensed with the background completely, giving total prominence to facial detail. Because of the BCU's potential dramatic impact, it should be used sparingly and with sensitivity.

VERY LONG SHOT/WIDE SHOT (VLS/WS)

These are usually used at the beginning of a sequence to establish the scene.

The human figure is relatively small in the frame, giving a general view of the surrounding environment/landscape.

LONG SHOT/MEDIUM LONG SHOT (LS/MLS)

This shot, a little closer in than the VLS, begins to isolate the subject in the frame. It contains the full figure, head to toes, and still includes much of the surrounding background.

MEDIUM SHOT/MID SHOT (MS)

The MS extends to just below the figure's waist, giving much more prominence to the figure and allowing room for hand movements and even the addition of another figure, making it a *two shot*.

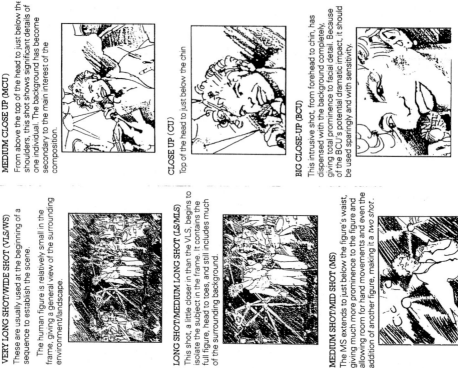

Fig 6.1

Source: The S4C Media Pack, S4C/MEW, 1989

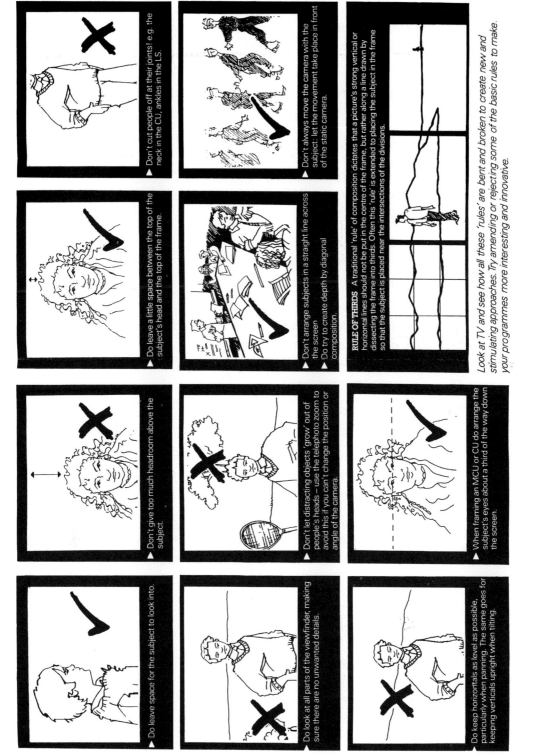

Figure 6.2

Source: The S4C Media Pack, S4C/MEW, 1989

He smiles at a group of people who return the smile, thinking that he has left his address and an apology. He drives off and waves. Later, the owner of the damaged vehicle returns, picks up the note and reads: 'I am writing this because people are watching me. Sorry I hit your car. Bad luck!'

Read through the story and decide how you would film it.

Tips
- Look at Figure 6.1 where shots are listed to help you.
- In what order will you put events?
- What gender/age should protagonists be?
- Will you film from one point of view or from several?
- Use Figure 6.2 to help you.

Task 3: Different style of treatment
You are going to make a film about your life or that of a relative. Make a plan of the events you wish to film.

Tips
- Order of events will be important. Flashback or chronological approach?
- One detailed event or a history?
- Voice-over or omniscient approach?
- One version or several?

Task 4: Studying a scene

Stage 1
Look again at 'North by North West' (1959) from the scene where Roger Thornhill comes to Vandamm's hideout at Mount Rushmore to the scene where Thornhill and Eve run to Mount Rushmore.

Stage 2
Make notes on the scene so that you can look in detail at the ways in which Hitchcock creates identification for the audience.

Tips
- Role of star
- Camera positioning
- Situation
- Audience knowledge
- Use of music or silence
- Creation of tension
- Use of setting.

Stage 3
You may wish to write up your notes as an analysis of the scene.

Investigating time and space

Time

Extra information

- In the short film 'Incident at Owl Creek' (1964), directed by Enrico, a Southern gentleman is about to be hanged from a bridge by Union soldiers. Suddenly, as he is about to die, the rope snaps and he falls into the water. Miraculously, he escapes the barrage of bullets, floats downstream, revels in the beauty of the world and gets back to his plantation where he sees his beloved wife approaching him. They run towards each other (a cinematic cliché) but as she reaches to put her arms around his neck we cut to the bridge where he is swinging, dead.

- The film is a piece of wishful thinking which extends the seconds of thought in the prisoner's mind before he dies to the minutes which make up the film.

- This short film illustrates the importance of time in the cinema. Time is relative and can be curtailed or extended as the director chooses. In this case, by entering the mind of the protagonist we experienced time as he did.

- Very few films operate in real time. 'High Noon' comes near to this by having the clock measure the time until the train bringing the avenger back arrives, but even here time is not strictly accurate.

- We accept the fact that in two hours a film can give us a whole life story or cover many years or just a few days. We willingly 'suspend disbelief'.

- When we see a character training for a mission it may take only a few seconds but we assume that what we see is symbolic of hours of training which would be boring to watch in reality.

- Similarly, a character may state an intention to go somewhere but if the journey is uneventful we do not see it but witness only their arrival at the destination. We do not want to see 'dead time' and we accept the conventions of time in the cinema.

Activity

Time.

Task 1

Read through the examples and see if you can add examples to those given from your own viewing. If you cannot think of examples now, jot them down in your notebook as you notice them in future.

Accelerated motion

This is obvious to spot because time moves quickly. It is often used for comic effects, for example in chase scenes. However, effects other than comic ones are achieved this way. For example in the film 'Return of the Jedi' (1983) the chase on speeder bikes was achieved by filming the scene slowly and then speeding it up.

See if you can spot this technique in other films.

Slow motion
Slow motion is often used to give special attention to an event. Dramatic events can be slowed down so that we do not miss the significance of them or balletic or athletic prowess can be emphasised by such an approach.

Can you think of a film which uses this technique?

Reversed motion
This is when an action is filmed and then played backwards. Everyone's favourite example is probably in 'Mary Poppins' (1964) when the nanny snaps her fingers and everything returns to the cupboards.

Stopped motion
Sometimes film-makers 'freeze' the frame so that there is no movement. This is used particularly in documentaries where only still photographs exist of a period or person. Sometimes a film starts with a still which 'springs to life'.

Each section of 'Meet Me in St Louis' (1944) starts with a photograph which then moves.

In 'Butch Cassidy and the Sundance Kid' (1969) the middle section of the film, where the characters visit a city, is told through still photographs and that film ends famously with a freeze-frame as the eponymous heroes run for freedom.

A similar technique is used at the end of 'Thelma and Louise' (1991).

Task 2

Extra information
- Time is closely related to montage or editing. 'Montage' is a term which tends to be used more in Europe and suggests the building up of a scene, whereas 'editing' is a more American word which suggests cutting a scene down. (Tip: Add to your earlier working definition.)
- Whichever way it is looked at, editing is closely related to time as the order in which we see things governs our responses.

Stage 1
Take a story you know well. It could be a Shakespeare play or a fairy story.

Write down the main elements of the plot.

Tip
Try to keep the plot simple and make sure that the key scenes are listed.

Stage 2
Take the list of events and decide **either** to order the events for filming, deciding how the film will be shaped **or** take one event and try to structure the filming of the scene from two different positions.

Tips
- Camera angles
- Order of events
- Time devices
- Use of viewpoint.

Space

Extra information

- You have already looked at the page of camera shots in Figure 6.1 but now we will consider them in more detail.
- The frame is as important in film as it is in photography or in comics. There is more to looking at space in cinema than simply examining shots.
- Compared with the human eye, a camera lens is a crude device. Your human eye is always adjusting perspective for you but in order to have similar effects the camera must be carefully set up to create angles and effects.
- To achieve the illusion of depth, the film-maker can choose a particular lens, for example deep focus lenses can give clear definition throughout the whole frame.
- Lighting can help to give a sense of depth by lighting up the back of the frame.
- Generally, it is the angle chosen or the movement of the camera around a person or object which gives a sense of depth.

Activity   **Space.**

Task 1

Stage 1
Look at the following lists of effects of space achieved in cinema.

Stage 2
See if you can add to the examples. If you cannot do this now, add to the list as you watch new films.

A sense of scale
One way of showing size is to place something big in a picture.

In 'Thelma and Louise' (1991) some of the filming is done in Monument Valley which gives a sense of the smallness of human beings in the landscape.

We saw a sense of scale in watching 'North by North West' (1959) where the heroes climb on Mount Rushmore, where there are symbols of American presidents, showing that they are defending America. However, the scale of their task is huge.

Distance
Close-ups bring us close to stars and suggest intimacy. On the other hand, if characters are opposed or in conflict, space can be put between them.

Illusions
The camera can make objects look huge, for example models by Harryhausen in films like 'The Golden Voyage of Sinbad' (1973), or shrink people, as in 'Honey, I Shrunk the Kids' (1989).

Angles
High angles can give a sense of many people or of authority or menace while low angles can make people appear cowering or subdued.

Object motivation
Where an object appears in the frame can give it significance. For example, in *film noir* films objects often have the same focus and importance as people, giving the *film noir* world an alienating effect where objects appear strange.

Key objects in close-up are given significance, such as the light-sabre of the Jedi or the wedding ring in 'The Sixth Sense' (1999).

Access denied
Sometimes the film-maker will give a misleading angle on an object or scene so as to bring about a surprise.

A good example of this is the ending of 'Planet of the Apes' (1967), where we hear the character played by Charlton Heston curse mankind before we are allowed to see what he sees which is in fact the Statue of Liberty, confirming that he is on Earth.

Other reasons for not showing us things could be that they are too horrific or difficult to film.

Task 2

Extra information
- As editing is to time, so is *mise-en-scène* to space.
- *Mise-en-scène* is about filling the frame and thus the space of cinema.

Star Wars – The Phantom Menace   *Source: © Lucasfilm Ltd.*

With a still camera, take a series of photographs which experiment with using space.

Tips
- Use the shot list to help.
- Do not just take photographs of what exists. Set up the effects you want using light, props, make-up, hair, clothes.
- It may be easier to give your photographs a theme, such as city life or relationships.

Task 3: Filming the book
Take a very short scene from a book you have studied or like (a page would be enough). **Either** produce a storyboard of the scene with detailed drawings **or** produce a screenplay which gives dialogue, camera shots, etc.

Tip
If you choose to produce a screenplay, you should look at examples. There are many on the market at the present moment.

Task 4

Stage 1
Look at the opening and the ending of 'Titanic' (1997).

Stage 2
Make notes on:

- the structure of the story (see Todorov);
- the roles of characters (see Propp);

137

- the use of space and time;
- the use of viewpoints.

Stage 3
You may wish to write up your notes as an analysis of the film.

Investigating selling films

Information

- Most of the films we see see started out as something else. For example, many films started as novels or dramas.
- In the 1990s there was a real interest in bringing novels to the screen, such as the work of Jane Austen ('Sense and Sensibility' (1995)) and Charles Dickens ('Great Expectations' (1997)).
- This makes sense because films are expensive to make and it helps if the audience already has a **foreknowledge** of the project and will want to see what film-makers have done to a famous book.
- Other sources for films are drama, so that film-makers sometimes turn to classical plays like those of Shakespeare ('A Midsummer Night's Dream' (1999)) or Oscar Wilde ('An Ideal Husband' (1999)).
- In the 1990s there was a trend to make film versions of television cult series such as 'The Avengers' (1998) or 'Mission Impossible' (1996). All of these versions partly depend on the audience having foreknowledge of the project so that the audience already has expectations of the film. This makes it easier to sell it.
- Occasionally, films come to the screen which have an original screenplay written only for this medium. A project like 'Good Will Hunting' (1997) was written for filming, as was 'Star Wars' (1977).
- When a film has such success as 'Star Wars' or 'Raiders of the Lost Ark' (1981) then the probability is that a series of films will be produced on the strength of the original's success. In such circumstances, the film creates expectations in the audience so that a new film is looked forward to with excitement. This occurred with the release of 'The Phantom Menace' (1999) which as a **prequel** to 'Star Wars' excited audiences by sparking off interest by its relationship with the original trilogy.

Working definitions

Audience foreknowledge

The knowledge the audience brings to a project and which film-makers can rely on, for example knowledge of genre, a best-seller or a star image.

Prequel

A film which starts before the most recent narrative and backtracks the story.

Activity   **Film origins.**

Task 1
Make a list of your 10 favourite films and jot down the origin of the story of each one.

Tips
- Novel
- Drama
- Original screenplay
- Television
- Cartoon
- Prequel or sequel.

Task 2

Stage 1
Choose a book or old television series which you think would make a good film.

Stage 2
Make a case for the film by:

- giving a brief synopsis;
- suggesting casting;
- picking out three key scenes which would film well.

Tip
Try to think about what type of film your project would make by comparing it with similar successes.

Investigating stars and genre
Extra information

- Earliest silent films did not have stars but as film developed the language of close-up and character, the studios began to see that stars could be an important marketing device which would entice audiences to the cinema.
- Early stars included Mary Pickford (the so-called 'American sweetheart') and Douglas Fairbanks Snr (an early 'swashbuckler').
- Hollywood also began to manufacture stars who would appeal to audiences and

every studio had its own group of stars who were contracted to work only at that particular studio, such as MGM or Warner Brothers.

Activity   Stars.

Task
Look at this list of names.

Stage 1
Can you match up the star to his or her real name?

⦿ John Wayne	⦿ Marion Morrison
⦿ Rock Hudson	⦿ Norma Jean Baker
⦿ Cary Grant	⦿ Roy Fitzgerald
⦿ Judy Garland	⦿ Frances Gumm
⦿ Tony Curtis	⦿ Archibald Leach
⦿ Marilyn Monroe	⦿ Bernie Schwartz

Stage 2
Why do you think the names were changed? What connotations do the new names give?

⦿ The name of a star was considered important as it carried connotations but appearance was even more important. In the Hollywood era (1930–50) it was expected that stars would be beautiful, attractive figures who were removed from ordinary life as glittering objects of desire. Once a star was contracted then make-up experts, hairdressers and dieticians would descend on the person, making the star a desirable product. Accents were not allowed and actors would work with speech therapists to iron out the accent so that stars spoke in quite an English style.

⦿ In modern times, stars have more freedom as we do not expect them to be so different from ourselves, so that stars such as Sandra Bullock are popular for their ordinariness. It is much more likely that actors will keep their original name as ethnic origins are more celebrated than disguised, for example David Duchovny or Arnold Schwarzenegger. Nonetheless, stars still sell films and although stars try to resist their image by taking a variety of roles, audiences often have an image of them which makes them return to films by that actor.

Activity Cont'd.

Task 2

Stage 1
Look at this list of stars:

- Nicholas Cage
- Brad Pitt
- Bruce Willis
- Catherine Zeta Jones
- Gwyneth Paltrow.

Write down three films associated with each star.

Stage 2
From this make a list of five characteristics which you associate with the star named.

A star always plays an aspect of their own image, so that although they may emphasise some part of their character more in one film, they still carry all of the audience's foreknowledge of other roles with them whatever part they play. For example, Nicholas Cage's manic side may be played down in a sensitive role but as an audience we always carry the knowledge of his possibilities with us.

Activity Genre again.

Extra information
- Once film was established, the Hollywood studios soon realised that another selling point for films was genre.
- Audiences tend to have favourite genre products, which they will return to see. Saying that a film is in the tradition of another film the audience liked is a strong selling point. Do you have a favourite genre?
- A genre is a type of film which can be recognised because it has typical characteristics such as characters, situations, settings, plots, themes and icons. One of the most popular genres of recent times has been science fiction.

Task: Genre discussion
Look at the following list and see if you agree.

We can recognise a science fiction film because of:

Characters
Star fleet captains, aliens, mad scientists, intrepid women etc.

Situations
Lost in space, a new experiment, an invention, etc.

Settings
Space ship, lab, futuristic city, etc.

Plot
Machine goes wrong, aliens invade, journey into space, etc.

Themes
Sense of identity, good versus evil, prejudice and fear.

Icons
Computer screens, futuristic weapons, metallic colours.

Task
There are many popular genres such as horror, thrillers, comedies and romances. What is your favourite? Make your own list based on the one above.

Sometimes stars and genres are closely associated with one another. In the past, John Wayne was associated with Western films and Humphrey Bogart with thrillers. In more recent times Schwarzenegger has been associated with science fiction and Bruce Willis with action movies. When this happens the film becomes easy to sell as a vehicle for star and genre.

Investigating posters and trailers

Information

- You have already looked at posters earlier in the book. Now we will examine film posters in a specialist manner.
- Two ways of getting attention for a film are the use of posters and trailers.
- Posters can be shown on billboards and outside cinemas and often appear in magazines.
- Trailers are used in the cinema to attract similar audiences to those attracted to the film on show. Some trailers appear on television and at the beginning of videos.
- Posters take a great deal of thought and are carefully constructed.

Activity   Analysing film posters.

Task 1
Look through the list below and see if there is anything you do not understand.
Use it to deconstruct the poster of a heavily publicised recent film.

Main subject
- status/appearance/star (age, clothing, style, hair, etc.);
- body language (facial expression, eye contact, activity, pose, etc.);
- photographic coding (framing, lighting, focus, angle, etc.);
- objects and background (motivation for inclusion, connotations, etc.);
- anchorage (words with pictures).

Design/layout
- use of colour;
- typography;
- use of space;
- graphic devices.

Persuasive techniques
- portfolio of genre characteristics;
- use of stars;
- expert witnesses of film criticism;
- promises of pleasure (connotations of enjoyment);
- mark of quality (film logo or director's name);
- figures of speech (puns, alliteration);
- advantageous promises (being 'in', lifestyle, etc.)
- rule of three (phrases or adjectives in threes: 'Brave, Bold and Brilliant'; 'Fat, Forty and Phoney');
- gaining attention (humour, shock, surprise);
- use of memorable slogan (e.g. 'In space no one will hear you scream', 'Nice planet, we'll take it').

Audiences
- demographic profile (age, gender, class);
- in terms of product, for example over 18, thriller lovers.

Task 2: Trailers

Stage 1
Trailers have their own style of introducing characters and key moments.

Choose a film you have enjoyed and plan a trailer.

Tips

●   Choose three key moments from the film.

●   Take three characters and find a phrase to sum them up.

●   Make three statements about the plot or genre.

Stage 2

You now have the ingredients for a trailer. Try putting it together. Concentrate on the script rather than the pictures.

Tip

It is intended that you should be writing the **voice-over** for the trailer.

Investigating other ways of selling

Extra information

●   Films are so expensive to make that it is big business selling them. In order to market them, distributors cannot rely on posters and trailers alone.

●   Here are some other methods used:

1. **Free publicity**. Stories about the filming of a project are often released to newspapers and magazines. Favourite techniques are rumours of a romance or quarrel between stars, a controversial scene, rivalry between actors or secrecy about the filming of a scene. All of these get the press and thus the public interested in a film.

2. **Music links**. Soundtracks of films can bring extra publicity, particularly if the theme tune becomes a hit and gets into the charts, allowing footage of the film to appear whenever the recording artist does. The Bond films are famous for their songs. Can you give examples of any others?

3. **Chat shows**. Stars and/or directors appear on various television programmes when a film is released, showing clips from the film.

4. **Film of the film**. Where special effects are involved films are sometimes made explaining how the main film was achieved, Since special effects can be a draw in themselves this interests the appropriate audience. Recent examples have been explanations of 'Titanic' (1997) and 'The Phantom Menace' (1999).

5. **Spin-offs**. These help create interest in a film project and range from pencils and mugs to figures of characters. CDs and print versions of stories are also popular. In the film 'Jurassic Park' in a scene of inspired marketing we have a shot of the Jurassic Park shop which sells the items we can buy in our own local shop. At the

release of 'The Phantom Menace' as well as figures, pyjamas, etc. it was possible to buy diaries of main characters and read the story from different viewpoints. Computer games are also popular spin-offs from films.

6. **The Net**. This is increasingly a site for selling films. It had a huge part to play in the hyping of the low-budget film 'The Blair Witch Project' (1999), allowing it to have a wider audience and release. Film trailers are very common, for example the famous 'Star Wars' trailer. It is also a major area for 'stars' and 'fans' to get together.

7. **Interviews**. Film magazines as well as television programmes often give interviews to film-makers and stars, allowing them to promote their latest film.

8. **Reviews and criticism**. A film review is concerned with a film as entertainment. Reviews appear in newspapers and magazines and give audiences an opinion on whether the film is worth seeing. These rarely go into depth but give some idea of plot, genre and the types of pleasure the product will bring. Film criticism is more serious in that it tries to interpret the film's meaning and how it fits into the body of a director's or star's work. Ideally, for success in the broadest sense, approval is needed from both.

9. **Glittering prizes**. Film festivals allow film-makers to compete and some competitions are very prestigious such as the Cannes Film Festival, the Oscars or the British Academy of Film and Television Awards. Such awards are a selling point for the actual film and for films to come. Their receipt can be a selling point, for example 'starring three times Oscar winner' or even 'Oscar nominated'.

7 POPSCAPES

Information

- Pop music gives fans tremendous pleasure and in return fans give allegiance to the stars they admire. A star like Michael Jackson can withstand gossip, rumours and even charges (admittedly dropped) because fans support their idols whatever happens.
- The way we react to pop music works on different levels.

> First of all, we may hear a particular song which appeals to us because the lyrics are close to our feelings at the time or simply because the music appeals to us. This involves self-identification with the song and artist but we still only have a loose affinity with the star. Later, we may come to look out for the records of that star, begin to collect them, to read about the star and even collect memorabilia. This would be usual behaviour for a fan. Only a few fans go so far as to imitate the star they admire. At its most extreme this can be seen in Elvis lookalikes or people who attend concerts imitating the dress and behaviour of the star. Whatever level of fan a person is, there is no doubt that being one brings pleasure and interest to life.
> Based on Andrew Tudor's *Classifications*.

- Although fans can dictate trends to a certain extent, the world of pop music is dominated by the big businesses such as Warner Brothers or EMI which promote and release records worldwide.
- Record promoters are always looking for new trends in music and many bands who start off as alternative groups working for small independent companies are signed up by the bigger companies once their style has been recognised and established.
- Musical genres are constantly being recycled as older songs are reworked and presented to a new audience. This attracts older audiences who recognise the song from another era and a new audience for whom the song is brand new.

Can you think of any old songs that have been re-recorded in the last five years?

- There are so many genres and sub-genres of music and each type has its ardent followers and fans. In the world of the pop business, chart music is the big moneyspinner but, as well as chart success, there are also album charts and specific area charts, for example country, jazz or rock.

- Even within pop music itself the genres of rap, reggae, house, blues and heavy metal attract their own fan bases.

- The Internet is alive with the sound of music! (If you have programs like Real Player or Real Jukebox you will be able to explore this phenomenon.)

You may wish to pause here and 'brainstorm' as many different types of pop music as you can in one minute.

- Music is very important to audiences as being a fan can help define a person's identity and this is particularly true in teenage years. It is said, usually jokingly, that our music collections say something about us as people.

- If you go to any music shop, especially one of the bigger chains such as Virgin or HMV, you will see that music is marketed for different audiences, for example rock, country, folk, easy listening, etc.

- Similarly, radio channels cater for different types of musical taste, with Radio 1 going for a chart audience and Radio 2 espousing older and more middle-of-the-road audiences.

- Despite some targeting of specific programmes there is limited media coverage for more specialist types of music, which is where the Internet scores so highly.

Working definitions

Lyrics

The words of a song.

Memorabilia

Things we keep to remind us of the past. Pop memorabilia can be worth money to fans and could include musical instruments, badges, T-shirts, tickets and programmes for concerts.

Activity   **You and your music.**

Task 1: Your collection
Make a list of the last five CDs or tapes which came into your collection. What do they say about your taste in music?

Tips

- genre;
- gender;
- titles;
- labels.

Have they anything in common or do you have a wide taste?

Task 2: Applying a theory

Revision information
The 'uses and gratifications' theory is useful for analysing our own consumer habits.

Remind yourself of the theory which suggests that we are not passive receivers of media products and that we buy them for:

- escapism and pleasure;
- a sense of our own identity;
- a sense of belonging;
- knowledge they will bring about the world.

Stage 1
Read the article on the Beatles album in Figure 7.1.

Choose your favourite song or album and apply the theory to the pleasures it gives you.

Stage 2
You may wish to write a similar article yourself. Try to be specific about pleasure, identity, etc. Think about what the music really means to you.

Task 3: Genre
Choose a type of music, perhaps from your 'brainstorm' earlier. Now write down some typical characteristics of the genre you have chosen.

Tips

- typical song title;
- typical name for a group or singer;
- typical fan. Draw the fan and label the fashions;
- you are creating a stereotype.

Extra tip
Do not worry if you are not good at drawing – make the task into a profile instead.

Free as a Bird

Jude Brigley compares the Beatles' recent release with a favourite media text

Tasks for you

Choose a media product and write about the pleasures it has brought you.

Read the article and identify the pleasures suggested, using 'uses and gratification' theory.

Write an analysis of Beatles images using sleeves and lyrics.

The ghostly voice of Lennon intones Free as a Bird, making me ponder the sentiments of the song. His voice is plaintive, rather than assertive: maybe that's why so many people rushed out to buy that record – out of nostalgia for an era when people actually felt that freedom of spirit. People talk a lot of rubbish about the sixties, of course, but one thing is clear to me: when I was young there was a feeling that anything could be achieved.

Some particle of that optimism still lives on in me now, an essential part of my identity. That is why one of my favourite media artefacts is the LP *With the Beatles*.

It's 1964 and I discuss the world with my friend Janice in the front room of her council house. We drink coffee and feel grown up to have our own ideas and our own taste in music. I look rather bizarre, as I have had my hair cut close to my head in the style of Julie Driscoll – a style which makes her look chic, but makes me look like a street urchin. Underterred, I am wearing a leather cap (even indoors) as I consider this to be the height of sophistication; unfortunately all my friends wear them as well.

On the Dansette floats Janice's Beatles record. I do not own it but I envy it. We play it again and again. We like the cover: the four faces in classy black and white with the polo neck jumpers seem to be staring at us as if to say *"we are young, we are free, we are working class and we can be successful"*. Sorry Supergrass fans, we've been there.

The sleeve has notes on the record. We have both read these a thousand times. Knowing all of these details is important: we like to be informed. Part of the pleasure of a record was to carry it around to a friend's house to play, or to borrow it yourself. Carrying it on the bus from Caerau, large enough for any young person to read your badge of identity, reading the cover notes on the bus, probing your intellectual interest.

And the music? That is another pleasure, but small in comparison with the object itself. Despite its occasional plaintiveness *(You really got a hold on me)* or brashness *(Money)* the overwhelming feeling is one of optimism. So in 1964 we sang along with *It Won't be long and Hold me tight* and our preferred readings were that these were more than love songs: they fed the feeling that life could be what you make it. That came back to me when I heard *Free as a Bird*: I wonder what Janice and my other old friends would make of that.

Figure 7.1

Investigating pop music on television

Extra information

- Considering the huge consumer interest in pop music, the television industry does not cater for musical taste very well.
- There are a few pop music programmes on terrestrial television and some channels on satellite but it is hard to classify pop programmes together as there are many different forms of programmes which deal with pop.
- Some concentrate on performance while others are more interested in personalities. The type of music will define the style of presentation, for example heavy metal stars are supposed to be loud and insulting. This can create a programme 'value'.
- Mainstream pop is dealt with by performance programmes like 'Top of the Pops'.
- Big events like rock concerts are covered by television but pop stars also appear on a whole range of programmes such as breakfast television, chat shows, etc.
- Specialised music tastes do not depend on television alone but on a range of marketing approaches including radio, music press, advertising, handouts and freebies.

Working definition

Freebie

Something which is given away in order to advertise a product or entice the audience to buy something. In pop, freebies could include posters, signed photographs or lapel buttons.

Activity   **Pop music on TV.**

Task
Imagine you were going to plan a programme for television, which dealt with an aspect of pop music. Think about the elements that would make an interesting programme.

Tips
- genres of music;
- name of programme;
- channel and channel 'values';
- running time;
- audience;
- typical people on programme: presenters, performers and audience;

- settings;
- typical items
- subject matter covered;
- icons by which programme would be recognised.

Investigating rockumentaries

Extra information

- Many of the programmes on pop music which appear on our screen are documentaries which give us information about stars and take us behind the scenes of pop concerts or give us interviews with our rock idols.
- When watching such programmes the same things apply as watching any documentary. Documentaries tell stories and you should remember that a story is always told from someone's point of view. When we tell a story we select and order events, choosing what to include and what to leave out. A documentary film-maker is exactly the same.
- For example, some documentaries claim to show a week in the life of a star. Since a programme usually lasts between 30 and 60 minutes, this is obviously untrue!
- To make the programme the editor has left out sections of the day and has decided what was important enough to leave in. Typically, this could be a star throwing a tantrum or quarrelling with a manager.
- Recent documentaries on Elton John and Gerri Halliwell have shown such scenes.
- Many people think that cameras and crew affect the way people behave. This could mean that we are not seeing things how they actually are because people find it difficult to behave naturally under observation.
- Modern film-makers sometimes rehearse dialogue with subjects and ask people to re-enact past events. Interviewees often have the list of questions they will be asked in advance, even though the interview is set up to look spontaneous.
- Most important of all, sound bites taken out of context or commentary can guide a response from the viewer which the events themselves would not prompt.

Working definitions

Rockumentary

A documentary made on a pop music subject, for example 'The Last Waltz' or 'This is Spinal Tap' (1984). The latter is a spoof of a rockumentary, based on a fictitious heavy metal group. This went so far as to be available on interactive CD-ROM with extra audio commentary on the film and out-takes.

Sound bite

A sound bite is a small amount of speech which has been recorded and which has been cut to a memorable sentence or phrase which can be quoted to sum up the thoughts or feelings of the interviewee.

Activity   Research.

Stage 1

Choose a star or group you admire or already know quite a lot about. Your task is to research them and find out as much about them and their style of music as you can.

You will summarise what you find out on one page.

Tips
- You can look in reference books and CD cover notes.
- Another source could be 'fanzines', if they exist.
- You could use the Internet.

Working definition

Fanzine
A magazine-type publication, often produced cheaply, which is distributed to fans and gives information on groups, interviews, etc. They are likely to be less frequently produced now that so many stars have web pages on the Internet.

Stage 2

Having done your research, you will be an expert on the subject. Imagine you are going to interview the person you have researched.

Tip

Do not worry if the star is dead as this is an exercise in imagination, so you could have chosen Elvis, Freddie Mercury or even Frank Sinatra.

Extra tips
- Start by listing suitable questions. You will need to think of the audience for this interview as this will dictate whether it will be serious or light-hearted.
- Look at examples of interviews on television.
- Look at the imaginary interview written by a student in Figure 7.2.

Stage 3
Rehearse and present the student interview.

Stage 4

You may wish to present your own interview as print or record it for radio or on video.

Investigating CD album covers

Extra information

- Since the fifties and sixties, album covers have been collectable items which reflect the music presented and often the art trends of the moment.
- Look at some CD covers you have and you will see that they have the following characteristics:

  a a cover design front and back;
  b inside photographs and credits;
  c sometimes words are printed;
  d sometimes there are notes on the artist or the performance.

- Covers play an important part in enticing us to buy and give pleasure at owning the object. Pictures of the stars often loom large on covers, attracting fans to buy, like on the Beatles album cover printed earlier in the chapter.
- Look at the cover of the 'Everything Must Go' album by the Manic Street Preachers in Figure 7.2.

Figure 7.2   Cover of 'Everything Must Go' by the Manic Street Preachers

Working definitions

Album

Originally a long-playing record, now a CD or cassette which has a collection of songs. Since the sixties these have sometimes been concept albums where songs are linked by themes or narrative. Single releases often come from albums as the same audiences do not necessarily buy both and those who do are genuine fans.

Credits

The names of people who worked on the album and their roles, for example sound engineers or musicians.

Manic Street Preachers album

- If we examine the Manics' album the first thing we would notice is that the background is a cool blue while the lettering is in black and red for contrast.

- The name of the group has several connotations. 'Manic' suggests frantic movement, a kind of madness and extreme emotion. 'Street' has connotations of credibility and of being of the people. We would expect the word 'fighter' to follow it and that connotation is still there in our minds. 'Preacher' suggests someone with a message and a particular role in society.

- The name of the group and the title are placed in a white rectangle edged with black, suggesting a street sign.

- 'Everything Must Go' suggests a sale but also carries the added connotation of revolution and change. It could be read as a statement or as a command. The parenthesis brackets are empty, creating a narrative enigma for the audience.

- The photographs appear to be propped up on a shelf like icons and the triptych effect (three panels) results in only the middle preacher looking at us directly.

- Their shirts of navy, black and white colour co-ordinate with the rest of the album cover.

- If you look inside the album cover inside, the 'shelf' idea is extended but the photographs deconstruct the artists into metonymic signs. (These are typical signs which sum up aspects of a subject.) In this case it is as though we are examining them in parts and as if life itself is being scrutinised in detail on this album.

● Something which is not reproduced here is the quotation from the American painter, Jackson Pollock, which is printed in the notes in large red letters:

> 'The pictures I contemplate painting would constitute a halfway state
> and an attempt to point out the direction of the future –
> without arriving there completely.'

The quotation shows that the band has serious intentions with its music.

Activity Creating a CD cover.

Task 1
Choose a CD from your collection and treat it to a similar approach to that above.

Tips
● name of group and album;
● key connotations;
● graphic designs;
● print;
● pictures;
● commentary.

Task 2
Create your own CD cover for an imaginary group, a compilation album, or a new album for an artist you admire.

Tip 1
● start with listing typical tracks;
● find a name for group and album.

Tip 2
● think about the images you will use;
● you could use montage, your own photographs or computer images to create the effect;
● if you are good at drawing you might like to create the design that way.

Extra information
Some singer/songwriters, like Joni Mitchell, have designed and painted all of their album covers.

Investigating pop videos

Extra information

- Pop videos are important in the marketing of music and have become a media form in their own right.
- You can buy compilations of pop videos, they are used extensively in marketing on television and sometimes attract film-makers to direct them because of the comparatively large budgets available for such a short piece of film.
- Thus, John Landis, the Hollywood director, worked with Michael Jackson on his 'Thriller' video, Derek Jarman, the British director, worked with the Pet Shop Boys and pop artist Andy Warhol worked with Curiosity Killed the Cat, among others.

Activity **Reviewing your pop history.**

Think of your five favourite videos (from the present and the past). Do they have any of the following elements?

- artists performing in studio or on stage;
- artists performing on the street as if the song was dialogue;
- a narrative structure which tells a story;
- scenes from a film interspersed;
- a journey;
- characteristics of a film genre;
- animation;
- images linked by the music;
- dance;
- something else?

Pop videos have many of these characteristics and in analysing them you will use many of the approaches you adopt for reading other moving images:

- narrative codes (enigmas, characters, structures);
- technical codes (lighting, angles, etc.);
- symbolic codes (connotations, symbols etc.).

Along with these approaches with pop videos you need to look carefully at star performance. The elements to concentrate on include:

- name;
- appearance;
- dress;

- objective correlatives (symbols, and objects which say something about the performer);
- audience foreknowledge;
- type of music and lyrics;
- movement.

Activity   Analysing pop videos.

Task 1
Choose a pop video you know well and, using the headings above, try to write an analysis of how it constructs meaning.

Tip
Watch the video three times, making notes under the headings before you write up your findings.

Task 2
Choose the lyrics of a song you know well and look at them in detail, taking notes on what you think the song means and what images it conjures up for you. Look at the connotations of the words.

Task 3: Making a video

Stage 1
Look back at the way students treated the poem 'First Ice' (Chapter 1).

Stage 2
Either:

Take a series of photographs illustrating the song and present it as a storyboard for a pop video. Once your photographs have been developed, do not hesitate to crop and use montage, drawings and colour to enhance presentation. Make an animatic and make the song fit your photographs.

or:

Storyboard the song. Film it on video.

- The song will need to be storyboarded carefully: think about *mise en scène*, location, etc.
- Keep your ideas simple and go for clear images.
- Edit carefully so that the images and music go together smoothly.
- Do not use too many tricks when editing. Remember the KISS rule: Keep it simple, stupid.

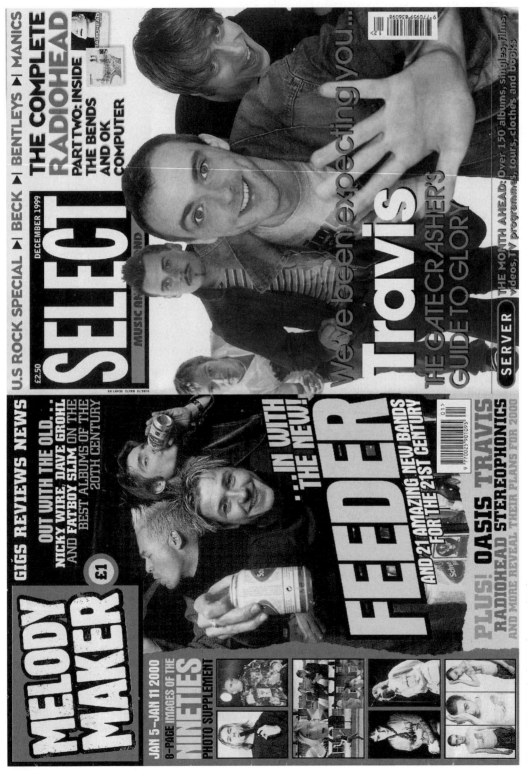

Figure 7.4 Melody Maker *and* Select

Investigating the music press

Extra information

- The music press can be very powerful in influencing audiences.
- Teenage girls' magazines such as *Sugar*, *J17*, etc. often feature chart music, giving interviews with 'heart-throbs' and role-models for young girls. This tends to be non-critical and based more on sex-appeal than the actual music.
- Newspapers and general magazines print reviews of new records or of concerts but the long-established *New Musical Express* (*NME*) and *Melody Maker* remain main sources of opinion on pop music. These tend to be aimed at 16 to 20-year-olds as they focus on current bands who are not likely to be of interest to an older generation.
- The music papers are distributed weekly and are therefore full of snippets of information, reviews and gig guides as they are by nature extremely up to date.
- Music magazines such as *Mojo*, *Select* or *Vox* are monthly publications and therefore tend to have more in-depth articles and interviews.

Activity **Music magazines.**

Task 1
Look at the advertising in a music magazine and list the things advertised.

What does this tell you about the relationship of the pop industry with 'lifestyle' advertising?

Task 2
Identify and collect glamourising references to sex and drugs.

What do these say about the music press's attitude to the industry ?

Task 3
Study the language used in the magazine. Make a list of swear words, slang, 'street language', etc. Does this say anything about the magazine's target audience?

Task 4
Compare the cover of the *Melody Maker* with that of *Select* in Figure 7.4.

Deconstruct the covers as you have for other magazines or posters.

What can you tell about the audiences of both?

Music magazines tend to be targeted at males. The papers are targeted at late teens while magazines such as *Q* were originally aimed at over 30-year-olds, though a large proportion of *Q*'s audience is under this age.

Task 5

Create a cover and a contents page for a new music magazine aimed at either women or a specialist music audience, for example jazz, rap or house.

Tips

- Think about a title, price and distribution.
- Use montage, drawing or computer images.
- Be sure to make your cover fit the conventions of a magazine front cover.

Task 6

Write an in-depth article for a magazine on an artist or style of music that interests you.

Tips

- Research (Other magazines? Typical fans? Fan sites? Artist sites? News groups?).
- Choose pictures (Cut and paste or download?).
- Write in an appropriate style for your audience (Read typical articles? Make lists of suitable words?).

8 SOUNDSCAPES: TUNING IN

Information

- Radio is a very personal medium. It addresses the listeners directly, as though they were acquaintances or close friends.
- It can provide entertainment, advise you, console you and cheer you up in much the same way as a friend does.
- It is a very portable medium. You can listen in very different locations and with different degrees of attention.
- Like friends, radio stations and programmes have different 'voices' and vary their tone and approach to the listener.
- Although much of the material on radio that most of you listen to is music, the main experience is communicated through words.
- Speech 'anchors' the music and sound.

Activity

Anchorage.

Choose your favourite song.

Task 1
Record a spoken introduction to the song to:

- someone who does not know the song;
- an older male;
- an older female;
- a fellow fan.

Tip
Change the words as well as the tone.

Task 2
Choose a radio station you listen to. Re-record your introduction to the song in a style appropriate to the station's output in:

- an early morning programme;
- a late afternoon show;
- an after-midnight slot.

Tips
- The audience will change.
- Your tone will change.
- The words you use will change.
- In each case try to visualise who you are talking to.

Activity The nature of radio.

What do you understand by each of the following statements?

- radio is a 'blind' medium;
- radio is a 'companion' medium;
- radio is an 'intimate' medium;
- radio is a 'flexible' medium;
- radio is an 'undemanding' medium.

Tip
Spider diagram your ideas.

Activity Branding.

Extra information
- The number of radio stations you can listen to is staggering, especially since the development of the Internet. A software programme like 'Real Player' lists hundreds of accessible stations.
- In 1994 nearly 100 local and regional stations were in operation in Great Britain alone.
- Everyone in this country can tune into whatever kind of radio station they prefer if they have the digital technology.
- Internet technology has given access to under-represented groups from across the globe. Radio stations in different countries can present a range of views on a conflict or event which are not mainstream, and have them on your desktop in seconds.
- Radio stations were in general much quicker off the mark in realising the importance of a distinctive identity for a station than was television.
- Independent radio stations cater for specialist audiences and attract advertising aimed at those audiences.
- This process is described as 'narrowcasting'.

Task

Flick through the radio stations you have available to you. List the ones:

- you recognise;
- you did not understand;
- you recognised but would never listen to;
- you did not recognise but you thought sounded interesting.

How much can you listen to?

Advanced group task

Identify the 'brand'.

Tips

- Name and logo.
- Key connotations.
- The major promises made to the listener.

Each group chooses an area for investigation from the following:

- the type of music played;
- the jingles and signature and theme tunes;
- news, traffic and weather bulletins;
- attitudes and accents of presenters: presentational styles (single person, pairs, etc.);
- scheduling profile: morning, afternoon, night;
- visual identity, as seen in logo, publicity material, posters in all kinds of locations.

Radio genres.

Extra information

Many radio genres have been transferred to television: news, documentary, situation comedy, quiz shows, 'talkback' and 'live' broadcasting of major sporting events, as well as popular ways of presenting music. As a consequence, they have a longer media history.

Activity   Interactivity and talk.

Extra information
- Radio stations have a long tradition of providing companionship to members of their listening communities.
- The 'talkback' show has been one of the most popular forms of interaction with the audience.
- Many films use the 'talkback' show as a part of their plot: 'Play Misty for Me' (1971), 'Pump Up The Volume' (1990) and 'The Fisher King' (1991).
- Many other radio genres have elements of 'talkback', especially current affairs.

Task 1: Where in the schedule?
- Choose a radio listings page.
- Choose a station.
- Identify programmes which have elements of 'talkback'.

Tip
Study the morning and late-night parts of the schedule first.

Task 2: Why do people need 'talkback' features?
Consider the following reasons and add observations of your own:

- to show off;
- to air their grievances;
- to get emotional support;
- to tell their story;
- to have a laugh.

Tip
Think about the use of the mobile phone in relation to this.

Task 3: The presenter

Extra information
- The mainstay of 'talkback' is the most topical event which has usually appeared in the news or in magazines. Often, depending on the programme's values, it is a bizarre, shocking or sensational story or a new survey on people's habits. In local broadcasting it will be appropriate to the station's audience.
- The presenter usually sets the agenda and invites people to call in.
- The presenter then controls the discussion in a variety of ways: questions, prompts, interruptions, etc., and finally has the ability to cut people off.

- The presenter looks to use callers to set up opposing positions to create a conflict or controversy. The aim is to create 'drama' or interesting listening.
- The presenter's style will be determined by the nature of the audience the show is hoping to attract.

Choose a talkshow and analyse the style of the presenter.

Tips
Use these categories to help:

- 'shock jock' style: shouting, insulting, taunting, showing up;
- authority figures: offer reassurance, common sense, balance, knowledge;
- chatty/gossipy/homely/good friend.

Activity Comedy.

Extra information
- Comedy is an essential ingredient of radio and appears in many guises.
- Language and sound are at the basis of comedy's appeal. If you love words, accents, funny voices, jokes and puns you will love radio comedy.
- Many television comedy programmes have their genesis in radio programmes.
- It is best to make humour rather than analyse it.

Working definitions

Situation comedy

> 'A sitcom is a light-hearted programme based on a single premise
> (a single parent in straitened circumstances, a group of friends who
> share an apartment) which provides the "situation". Sitcoms feature a
> cast of established characters who interact within a limited
> number of recognisable settings.'
> Stuart Price

Absurd parody or sketch comedy
- Series of sketches or skits or gags.
- Leaps from one sketch to another.
- Surreal, bizarre, black, alternative.
- Copies existing forms but with a new twist or from a different point of view: upside down and inside out, often.

Variety or stand-up comedies
- Loosely scripted, scripted or improvised dialogue: quips, gags.
- Can be single, in pairs, or in teams.
- Often in quiz-show format.

Humorous elements
- Stereotypes. Instantly recognisable from the voice or catchphrase or musical motif or typical saying.
- Expectation. The key to good comedy is making the audience wait. Timing is the essence of humour.
- Entry into a strange world through some startling event.
- Logical sequence of events from there. Every element has a reason or purpose which escalates the action into chaos and finally clinches it in a satisfying manner.
- Familiar narrative structure:

1. Initial proposition: a duck walks into a pub.
2. Complications: the duck asks for a drink and gets into conversation with the landlord.
3. Resolution: what's the punchline?

- Laughter and tears. Comedy usually has a range of emotions but in the end creates the sense that all will be well.
- Triumph and humiliation. Comedy is often cruel and people often get their come-uppance
- Incongruity: animals with human characteristics, men dressed like women, women dressed like men.
- Surprise: puns, malapropisms (Del Boy is a good television example), *doubles entendres* ('Carry On' films are good examples. Many of the 'stars' appeared on radio first).
- Sound effects. A splat or fart still creases many people up.

Task: Plan a comic talkshow

Tips
- Choose your audience.
- Choose your presenter.
- Choose the subject.
- Choose your callers.
- Plan your approach to include:

a a silly subject;
b silly answers;

c silly voices;

d lots of sound effects;

e a studio interruption.

Activity Radio drama.

Extra information

⦿ Major types:

a soaps started as a radio form ('The Archers' is the longest-running British example);

b factions (mixtures of fact and fiction);

c dramatised reconstructions of historical events;

d adaptations of famous novels;

e adaptations of stage plays.

⦿ You can use scripts in radio drama – no need to memorise the lines.

⦿ Rapid turnover times available.

⦿ No concerns about the weather or the light.

⦿ You can change location at any time.

⦿ You can change the historical setting.

Task 1: Researching types

Use a listings magazine to identify:

⦿ soap operas, one-off dramas, novel adaptations (serials) and their titles;

⦿ where they were produced;

⦿ radio station;

⦿ scheduled time of transmission.

Task 2: The role of the narrator

⦿ Introduces and establishes.

⦿ Introduces characters.

⦿ Describes settings.

⦿ Takes a part in the play.

Stage 1

Write and rehearse a narrative introduction to a play located in your school or college. It will last for 10 seconds only. (Rehearse with a stop watch!)

Stage 2:

Change the script to make the introduction come from the point of view of a character in the play.

Stage 3:

In three seconds introduce your main character in words.

Task 3: Montage

- Some dramas do not have a narrator.
- Characters are juxtaposed.
- Sounds are juxtaposed.

Stage 1

Tell a story using recorded snatches of real people's speech.

Stage 2

Tell a story using only sound effects. You could use sound effects records or tapes or download sound files from the Web.

Task 4: Dialogue

- Dialogue in plays is rarely, if ever, in sentences.
- Accents give instant information about a character.

Write a brief snatch of dialogue which shows the difference between:

- a young person and an old person;
- a farmer and a visitor to Britain;
- someone from Wales and someone from London.

Tip

You will use traditional stereotypes unless you are very cute!

Task 5: Soliloquies

- These allow us into the consciousness of a character who appears to speak directly to the audience.
- Their thoughts, fears, anxieties and dreams can all be explored by the writer without having to visualise them. It helps the listener to get closer.
- Many people prefer radio adaptations to television adaptations because of this ability to be close to the character.

Activity   **Voxcops: Dick Tective.**

Extra information

- High up in an office block on 'Tirdty Tird' Street lies the headquarters of PINY – Private Investigators of New York.
- Here we find our hero, Dick Tective, stuck in a time warp of 1930s America.
- So, grab your coat and take a trip down the mean streets.
- Look at Figure 8.1.

Figure 8.1

Task 1: The 20-second pitch
Using the following script, make your pitch to a producer of radio drama:

Taking his usual nightly stroll, Dick Tective stumbles across a mysterious body.

Dick vows to track down the killer after a mysterious blonde hires him to solve the murder. She will pay anything.

Confronting New York characters such as Baby Face Roberts, the bouncer, and Billy Buster, the owner of the local burger bonanza bar, Dick defies the odds stacked against him.

Murder, mayhem, kidnapping and the odd bad joke abound as Dick, the man from PINY, has you crying for more.

Task 2: An episode
Look at Figure 8.2 and write a script for the pilot episode.

Figure 8.2

Activity   Advertising on radio.

Extra information

- Commercial radio depends on advertising.
- It is inexpensive compared to advertising on film and television.
- You not need certain light or weather conditions.
- Actors can play different characters using a variety of accents.
- You can go to far-off lands without leaving the studio.
- It is harder for the listener to 'zap' when in the middle of a favourite show.
- The last thing you hear when you go shopping might be an advertisement. (NB Getting TV adverts close to the audience is being used in some shopping centres and malls.) The reason is selling at the point of sale.
- Prices for advertisements vary according to the time they go on air.

Figure 8.3

● Remember that radio 'narrowcasts': the target audience is critical to the advertiser.

Task: Local commercial radio

Stage 1
Find out about Cardata from the website address given in Figure 8.3.

Stage 2
Study the comic advertisement for Cardata. (It came from a petrol station receipt!)

Advise Cardata, as a potential advertiser on your station, on the best ways of attracting the kind of people the product or service is aimed at.

Tips

- Know the product or service: what is its key selling point?
- Grab attention instantly: music, jingle or first words?
- Hold the interest: people talking is the basic technique. (Extra tip: use your work on speech bubbles from your work on comic narrative.)
- In the dialogue, create a problem.
- Then create a solution.
- Then create action: what next?

Write and perform the radio script for Cardata.

Advanced discussion essay

Do you prefer the film version or the radio adaptation of one of Shakespeare's plays? Explain your reasons.

9 GAMESCAPES

Information

- The computer game industry was the fastest-growing media industry at the end of the twentieth century.
- Any shopping centre or mall in Great Britain now has a games store.
- Specialist magazines have been launched on the back of their popularity.
- Television stations devote programmes to reviewing and testing new products (for example 'Gamemaster', Channel 4, 1999).
- A key feature of the games is that they are interactive and players can be linked up to other gamers.
- Players communicate and get more information from the Internet through manufacturers' websites, the chatrooms they sponsor and organise and the fan pages which spin off from them.

Why is it important to study computer games?

- You can explore the importance of animation in modern media systems.
- Game play, especially among young males, has been a matter of concern: the role of games in the lives of students has led to all kinds of fears.
- Female representation, in particular, has been a focus of concern for some people.
- There are strong links between television cartoons, videos and advertisements; animated films and special effects; comic characters; and game situations.

Activity   Types of computer game.

Extra information
- Computer games are developed for a variety of audiences.
- They evolved in the 1990s at a phenomenal rate as digitalisation made the games more sophisticated, gave them better graphics and made them portable and quicker to run.
- They are experienced in a variety of ways by the audience.

Task 1: Discussion
Add your observations and examples to these simple categorisations.

Make them more complex.

Stage 1: Working definitions of types
Arcade – Paid for when used. Simple, action-style narratives or quizzes. Easy-to-use interfaces. Short play times. Situated where people congregate: motorway service stations, town centres, pubs and cafés.

Racing games – Simple, narrative action. The interface is easy to use. Often a simple steering wheel and gear stick.

Simulations – Often very complex as they need to be realistic and believable. Often to do with war, flight or sport. Can be strategy and planning (as in 'SimCity').

Combat games – The most popular genre. Strong links to movies, television programmes and merchandising. Complicated controls and sophisticated movements by the user. Use of levels to increase the challenge. Can have a variety of formats: PC, platform, hand-held.

Role play – Complex narrative structures. Global dimensions via the Internet. Narrative interaction. Navigation of levels is a central feature. Often use 'a point of view' interface (PoV), i.e. you get to choose who or what you will be.

Stage 2: Typical narrative structures
On the whole, games have typical narrative structures.

- The set-up and initial problem (place, characters and equipment). Short, generally.
- The journey (complications, trials, tests, helpers and opponents). Main section.
- The resolution (often very quick, and the shortest stage). Often signalled by a sound effect or message.

- Stereotypical characters: tend not to develop initial characteristics but reinforce them in a variety of circumstances.
- Stereotypical settings: islands, dungeons, castles, space, buildings.
- Screen elements: status bar (health, ammunition, objects collected, time, etc.) is most common. Often reinforced by auditory cues.

Task 2: Design
Design posters to illustrate your findings.

Tips
- Use montage techniques.
- Download suitable images from the Internet.

Activity **Investigating female representations.**

Task

Stage 1: Collecting examples
Study a selection of comics, games and animation. Explain how you could work out whether they were for a female or male audience. (Use the following categories to help you: damsel in distress, sexy sidekick, victim, onlooker, leader and heroine.)

Stage 2: Examine the 'heroines' in more detail
- Consider whether they are a 'good' representation of a female character.
- Do they appeal to a female audience?
- List the different kinds of heroines.

Consider:

- facial features;
- poses;
- the way they dress (or not !).

Stage 3
Study the representations in Figure 9.1 of two famous women characters from the 1990s: Battle Angel Alita and Tank Girl. Comment on the significance of:

- name;
- appearance;
- props;
- poses;
- eyes.

Figure 9.1

Stage 4
Who in your group would take up Tank Girl's invitation?

Activity Media effects.

Many groups have expressed concern about the effects of games on young people.

Key criticisms
1. They encourage aggressive behaviour. They show extreme violence. To be successful, the player is encouraged to use force. Players are likely to imitate this violence in real-life situations.
2. They are addictive and time-consuming. They replace other more physical activities (like sport) or mental activities (like reading).
3. They isolate players and encourage them to be solitary and uninterested in the social environment.
4. They are repetitive and can create a health hazard to eyes especially, hands and backs.

Some researchers have found positive benefits.

Key benefits
1. Players enjoy the challenges and puzzles presented by the game narratives.
2. Games encourage the kinds of skills and abilities required in the new technological age.
3. Games are shared, played in groups and the merits of particular games endlessly discussed.
4. Games for most young people are a part of a full and complex life. Children love all sorts of things passionately for a time. Some become 'fans' who in turn become experts and make a living out of their expertise.
5. There is very little evidence to support the idea that these games produce aggressive attitudes and behaviour in real life. They are certainly an important part of 'play', whether in the form of bows and arrows or pretend lasers or karate kicks.

Task 1: Targeting the consumer
Study the visual resources on NeoGeo in Figure 9.2.

Stage 1
Explain the ways in which it markets itself.

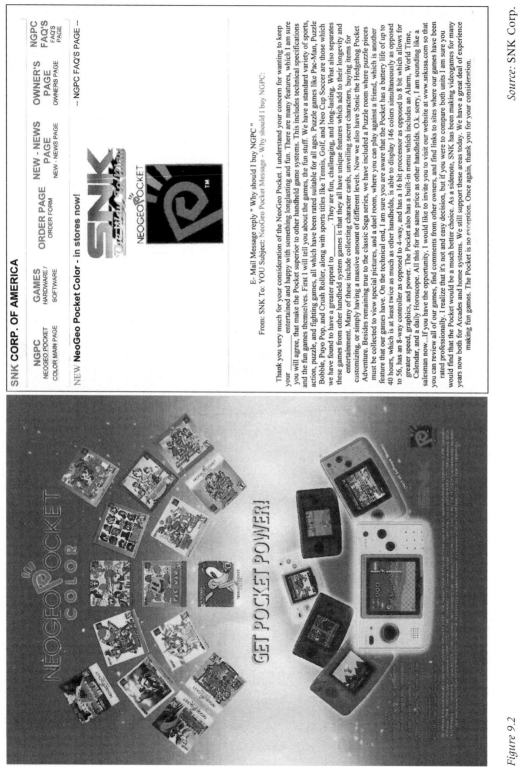

Figure 9.2

Source: SNK Corp.

Tips
- Text-mark the material.
- You could download colour copies!

Stage 2
Explain some of its advantages for the consumer.

Task 2: The individual consumer
Study the following interview between Mike Edwards and Cassian Marriner-Edwards, aged nine, from Wiltshire. (See Figure 9.3.)

Tip
Q = Mike Edwards

A = Cassian

Figure 9.3

Q. When was the first time that you heard about these hand-held computer games?

A. I first had this hand-held game for the PlayStation that you could pop the memory pod in. We went to the shop to buy another one ... the man sells them and he said 'If you are looking for hand-held games then there is this that's out and it's called NeoGeo ... it sounded quite good. I asked if it was like the Nintendo Game Boy. He said it was ... kind of ... but it is probably better.

Q. So what is the advantage for you? You have a PlayStation too. You play with your friends with that. What is the advantage of the NeoGeo for you? [See Figure 9.4.]

A. You can travel around with it and can also have a lead that you can connect to another NeoGeo so you can play with your friend who has the same game.

Q. Do you swap games as well?

A. You can if you want to but I wouldn't.

Q. What games have you got?

A. I have 'Metal Slug', 'King of Fighters R2', 'The Mini Puzzle Game' and 'The Pocket Tennis'.

Q. Which do you think is the best one?

A. Either the 'King of Fighters' or the 'Mini Puzzle'.

Q. Do you have discussions with your friends about which is the best?

A. Sometimes but there is only one friend who has one because they are quite new and not many people have them.

Q. Do you try and persuade other people that they are a good thing to have?

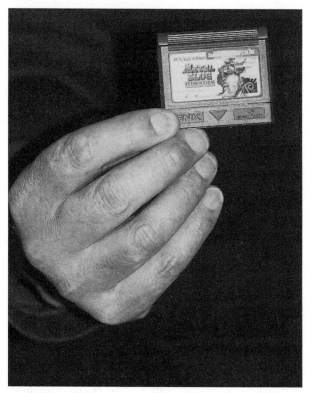

Figure 9.4

A.   Yes.

Q.   *What do you say to them?*

A.   I show them the games and they play on them and then they really get into it because they have never seen them before.

Q.   *What are the main things that they see that are different from what they have seen before?*

A.   The graphics are quite nice. The games are quite good.

Q.   *What is a typical game that they like that they have not seen before? What are the special ones that you would show to people and say, 'this is an example of why you must have NeoGeo'?*

A.   The 'King of Fighters' has been a big hit with all my friends.

Q.   *What would you say a hit was? What are the things in it that make it a hit?*

A.   Something that has a lot of action in. When I got the set I went for the action kind of games.

Q.   *Do you want to be the person in the computer games? Would you like to be a character? What is your favourite character?*

A.   Probably 'Kaio' in one of the games.

Q.   *What is he like?*

A.   He wears a blue uniform, has quite big eyes, has nice hair and is a fighting person who does lots of special moves … just like magic.

Q.   *Who are the enemies?*

A.   There isn't really one enemy but he just fights against other people so you don't walk around and try to jump over these things. There is a lot of fighting.

Q.   *Do you have to get better to progress?*

A.   Yes. There is a certain bit where you have to play the Master to get through. There is a making part of the game where you can decide what special moves you want to do. That's the fun bit and I have completed it. It's a really good game.

Q.   *What about the price of these games? Are they expensive?*

A.   I think they are a lot cheaper than Nintendo Game Boy ones because some of the Nintendo games are £30 but most shops do these for £25 each but I am a member of the MVC. That is a computer game shop where if you have a card you can get games cheaper. For about £3 less.

Q.   *Do they send you a newsletter?*

A.   No. You just ask for a card and give them your name and address. They don't send you anything or get a badge, you just have the card.

Q.   *Do you prefer this kind of hand-held game?*

A.   I prefer the PlayStation because there is a lot more action and it has better graphics. But I must say if you do want a mini and the PlayStation is getting boring I would play on the NeoGeo. You don't get that bored as you can change more often.

Q.   *Is it an advantage to be able to do it anywhere you like?*

A.   Yes.

Q.   *What's the wackiest place you have played?*

A.   Only in the car, which is normal really, but I could play at 2'o clock in the morning in a stop-over.

Task 3: Survey work: Consumers as groups

Stage 1
Explore Years 7, 8 and 9's use of computer games.

- Plan a series of prompt questions which you will use.
- Make sure you include girls and boys in your focus group.
- Here are some questions to get you started:
  1. Range of comics read?
  2. Games played?
  3. Favourite games?
  4. Favourite animated cartoons?
  5. Time spent on games?
  6. How much money do they spend?
  7. What effects does it have?

- Get the focus group together, using your teacher to help.
- If you can record the group's discussion, so much the better. If not, take careful notes.

Stage 2
Analyse your findings by using the following questions:

- What did the group know about comics, animation and games?
- Did they know the terms 'Manga' or 'anime'?
- What ways of involving themselves with other people were there?

- Do games get in the way of playing with their mates?
- Did they feel violent content in such games was an issue?
- Was gender stereotyping a big issue for them?

Stage 3
Present an audio report to your class, using 'sound' quotations from your material.

Activity

Textual analysis: The jewel case.

- These are a key marketing device at the point of sale.
- They are intended to be looked at and picked up.
- They need to be displayed.

Look at Figure 9.5 and use the following questions to help you to deconstruct the two game jewel case inserts.

How are the inserts constructed?

Figure 9.5

Tips

- Blow them up on a photocopier!
- Use the front cover, spine, back cover.
- Think about stereotypes, characters, the words used, the narrative and genre.
- Think about the slogans. What is the message? Think about how the organisation wants the customer to respond.
- What is the target audience?

Explain how the elements have been constructed to encourage you to buy. Go on to explain which, in your view, was the most successful.

Activity   The controversy.

Extra information

There is an enormous amount of 'talk' about computer games and their effects, especially on the young male.

Study the web page from Totalgames in Figure 9.6 and respond to it.

WWW.TOTALGAMES.NET   *NEWS*

Drugs Tsar Condemns Videogames?

"Computer games could be responsible for turning young people on to drugs because they no longer know how to make their own fun, Britain's drug tsar warned yesterday." Taken from '<u>Computer kids driven to drugs'</u> by Kirsty Walker, Social Affairs Correspondent, The Express Newspaper (online archive, http://www.lineone.net/express/00/01/11/news/n24–d.html)

This sensational opening paragraph is the beginning of an article featured in the Daily Express yesterday. The man behind these comments, the British Drugs Tsar is Keith Hellawell. The article has sparked outrage and incredulity from many areas, not to mention, rebuke. Tom Whitwell, editor of Club magazine 'Mixmag' was quick to reply;

"These comments confirm that Mr Hellawell has lost touch with anyone under the age of 45 in this country."

The games industry is not only a growth industry in Britain, but currently generates more revenue than video rental or cinema and is snapping at the heels of sell through video and music as Britains premier entertainment industry. In 1998 the retail value of consumer software was £890 million.

Indeed the insinuation that playing computer games leads to drug abuse is inflammatory to say the least. We decided to contact the Cabinet Press Office to find out whether Keith Hellawell was indeed some kind of lunatic in a high position.

A spokesperson for the Cabinet Press Office was kind enough to enlighten us over the 'misunderstanding'. He told us that The Express had not quoted Mr. Hellawell directly, and suggested that they had sensationalised his comments.

What Keith Hellawell was trying to do, apparently, was ask the gathered reporters why the children of today—who he described as the 'computer game generation'—were turning to drugs despite the availability of so much other stimuli. With computers, the Internet, games, literature, movies, sport and the plethora of other stimulating past-times, why were they still turning to drugs? The spokesperson also went on to say that Mr. Hellawell was keen on tackling all drugs, not merely the illegal ones. I.e. Alcohol, Tobacco and prescribed drugs.

In light of the explanation from the Cabinet press office, the finger points to media sensationalism by the Express newspaper. If Keith Hellawell really has to ask such questions however, one has to wonder why this man is a Drugs Tsar. Perhaps it's indicative of governments continuing tradition of ignorance and hypocrisy when it comes to drug related matters.

I want to urge **TGN** readers, especially if they fit the description of the so-called disenfranchised, drug-taking computer game generation, to share their views on this subject with us <u>here</u>. If you are in the UK you may wish to even wish to write to your MP and tell him your opinion on the appointed Drug Tsar of Great Britain.

written by <u>Sney Noorani</u>,
TGN News Editor

 NEXT

Figure 9.6

Activity   TombRaider and the cyber heroine.

Task 1: Promotion on the Internet
Analyse some elements of the Eidos website. Explain what the site offers the browser.

Tips
- Products
- Information
- Merchandise available: comics, toys, mousemats, screensavers, books, films, new games.

Activity   The star system.

Extra information
- Lara Croft is the public face of TombRaider.
- She has been the front cover model for magazines and has been used for publicity stunts.
- She even has a human equivalent who is used in the promotion of the game at trade fairs.
- She is a very familiar icon who is instantly recognisable and has a following of fans.
- She is a global phenemenon.

Task 1
Study the Eidos homepage. Explain the ways in which it creates Lara Croft as a global icon.

Task 2: The star as a media production

Stage 1
Download photographic images of Lara Croft from the Eidos website.

Stage 2
Deconstruct the 'star' image as follows:

- the pose of the star and setting of the photograph
- the style of the image, for example black and white or colour? why?
- facial expression
- costume/hair/make-up
- body language.

Stage 3
Consider the following:

- her name and its connotations
- her image (the female Indiana Jones)
- the audience's expectation of her.

Stage 4
Study 'The Official Lara Site' and evaluate:

- her profile
- the kind of publicity she gets
- the type of magazines she is advertised in and who buys them (*Loaded, GQ, Essential PlayStation*)
- the game
- use of animated sequences of action in the game
- the new hand-held game.

Activity **Make your own animated female for the millenium.**

Task 1: Constructing the new heroine
Ask yourself these questions:

- Would she be like the representation of Lara Croft?
- What would be your key elements?
- Where would these elements come from: the past, literature, films, computer games, comics, television, pop music,dance, the theatre?

Tips
- Revise the work on television characters (in Chapter 5).
- Make a profile like the one on the Official Lara Site.
- Do some concept sketches.

Task 2: Challenging women 1

Extra information
- Lara Croft is a women with a weapon.
- She clearly clearly draws on a set of narrative conventions to do with powerful female protagonists.
- Other media characters such as Emma Peel from 'The Avengers' (ITV, 1960s), Ripley from the 'Aliens' series of films, 'La Femme Nikita' (C5), the Kabuki comics, 'Xena: Warrior Princess' (C4).
- Conventions associated with new media heroines include:

1. Special skills: martial arts expert, explosives expert, can dematerialise.
2. Appeal to a female audience: smart, very intelligent with a sharp sense of humour.
3. She is most often young.
4. She is marked out from society. Something has changed her which makes her choose this kind of lifestyle: the death of her family, loss of a loved one, etc. She has moved from a secure life to an adventurous one.
5. She enjoys risking life and limb in the name of a good cause.

Stage 1
Brainstorm ideas about the representation of 'animated' women using this new evidence.

Stage 2
Discuss the idea of women as the audience and whether their needs are being met by the media.

Stage 3
How does the class respond to existing 'heroines' in the broadcast media – TV drama, films, adverts?

Stage 4
Is the 'new' heroine really 'new'?

Stage 5
Should there be more games, comics and animation for the female audience?

Task 3: Challenging women 2

Extra information

Villains have proved to be as important as the heroes and heroines in recent years. Can you think of any examples?

Stage 1
Create a worthy animated male adversary for your 'new' animated woman.

Tips
- Name
- Appearance
- Speech
- Biography
- Key moments of his life

- Choose some media stars to model the character on.

Stage 2
Create a 'new' animated female adversary.

Tips
- Does she have a code name?
- Where is she from? What's her history?
- How does she speak? Does she have an accent?
- How is she evil? What are her motives?
- How does she dress?
- What are her special skills?
- Which star would you choose to play her in a film version?

Advanced Activity

Write an essay: 'Can animation develop your understanding of the concept of "representation"?'.

Tips
- Think about 'media construction' and the idea that in animation anything is possible (just about!).
- Think about the ideas of 'typicality' you have explored.
- Use examples from your own work.

10 SPORTSCAPES

Information

- Like all media output, the coverage of sport is a representation. Selection and construction procedures are evident in all areas of the coverage. Events are interpreted for us and presented to us from a particular point of view.
- Television is central to sport. Without the coverage many minority sports would struggle for recognition and without the sponsorship deals many major sports would have been financially ruined.
- Radio allows for greater flexibility in sports coverage because it can convey the drama of several events during the same programme.
- Radio sports coverage contains a sense of narrative progression. The commentators appear to be telling us a story with highs and lows, periods of suspense and periods of triumph.
- Sport has a regular slot in most broadcast news bulletins and all media institutions have regular sports correspondents.
- Sport has always been a major element of newspapers and magazines. The growth of specialist sports magazines in the 1990s follows the trend to diversification of titles aimed at different kinds of audiences in the magazine sector.
- Advertising and sponsorship of sports and sporting competitions is a central feature.
- The Internet is increasingly being used as a major means of promoting and sustaining the sports audience: sports organisations' pages, media companies' pages, fan pages, live events and interviews, chat rooms, bulletin boards and news groups, fanzines, results, reports and expert views. The Web is alive with sport.
- Sport is often transmitted 'live' from a range of outside broadcast (OB) units. The broadcasters' aim to offer the consumer 'the best seat in the house' and the experience of 'being there where the action is'.
- 'Live' is a key sports 'value'.
- Live commentating has become a specialist profession.
- Many sports teams and individual personalities rely on sponsorship deals for their very existence.
- Who sponsors your local football team? What about your younger brother's or sister's favourite football team?
- One man, Rupert Murdoch, has had a huge impact on the world of televised sport. His media empire spreads from the United States to Europe, Asia and Australia. His global corporation has influenced fixtures to fit in with scheduling, encouraged

people to buy satellite receivers and made millions out of the 'pay-per-view' concept for specialist events. This means huge investments in technology and, therefore, to spread the investment many media companies need to diversify their interests (as Disney has done). Murdoch has introduced new technologies, newspaper price-cutting, the move to snappy 'tabloid' values and, because of his global span, has challenged national broadcasting systems all over the world. His impact is so great because he actively pursues a policy which draws different kinds of media together in one large umbrella organisation. He controls newspapers, magazines and television stations and owns shares in sports organisations.

- Media organisations have become businesses devoted to profits for shareholders. Sport has become even more cross-media than before. It crosses the boundaries of all of the entertainment media.
- Sport is a huge, global media phenomenon.

Activity

Your encounters with media sport.

Task: Developing a viewpoint.

Stage 1
List the sports do you think feature most often on television and radio Why do you think this is?

Stage 2
What minority sports have you encountered on television and radio? Synchronised swimming or curling, perhaps?

Stage 3
Are there any sports you can think of that have never appeared on television or radio? Can you explain the reasons for their absence?

Stage 4
Can you define what actually constitutes 'sport' in the broadcast media?
The lists you will have made in response to the two previous questions are likely to be very diverse and yet they are all sports. What is their common link? Why do you think some are more popular than others?

Stage 5
How is sport made attractive to audiences who comprise a range of individuals who have no real interest in participating in sports activities themselves?

Stage 6
Does sports coverage fuel nationalistic feelings? Consider the flag waving, draping of flags and face painting at major football and rugby matches or at the

Olympics. What do you think could be the consequences of these activities? Racial abuse? Stereotyping? Control?

Stage 7
Should one corporation control so much of the world's sports broadcasting? Use either the Internet or the most recent edition of *The Guardian Media Guide* to log the extent of Rupert Murdoch's News International's influence

Activity   The range of sports coverage on radio and television.

Task 1

Stage 1: Analysis
Analyse a current issue of the Radio Times and make a list of the sports covered on terrestrial radio and television over a three-day period (Friday, Saturday and Sunday).

Stage 2: Evaluation
- Are there any surprises? Are there any sports featured that you didn't know were covered by the mainstream media?
- Are the sports more male- or female-oriented?
- What conclusions can you draw about gender bias in media sports coverage?

Stage 3: Women in sport
Use the Internet to find out as much as you can about the Women's Sports Foundation. How does it attempt to raise interest in women's sports? Consider:

- images (visual/sound);
- text;
- advertising;
- links.

Task 2

Use a listings guide to consider the range of sports offered by satellite and cable stations. What are the main differences between terrestrial and satellite/cable stations in the sports and events covered?

Gary Lineker   *Source: © Doug Peters (All Action)*

Activity

Analysing a televised sports presentation.

Task 1: 'Announcing'

Stage 1
Note the scheduling details for the programme (when, where, time, nature).

Stage 2
Comment on the audience expectations that are being raised by the title sequence and introduction. Consider:

- music;
- 'sting' (the reminder to the audience of the television 'brand');
- framing;
- presenters.

Task 2: The coverage

Stage 1
Study the positioning of the cameras. Consider how many are being used and what aspects of the event each one is concentrating on.

Try drawing a plan of the location and marking in the fixed camera positions.

Stage 2
Consider 'mobile framing' and its area of operation.

Task 3: The commentary
Make notes on the commentary.

Tips

● Does it have a clear sense of narrative progression? The commentator is likely to 'fill in the gaps' during the more mundane moments of the game by giving the audience background information. This will have been well researched and will give an insight into the team players.

● How does the commentator deal with the blend of background information and commentary on the live events that are occurring?

● Who is actually speaking? Is it always the commentator or are there personalities or experts helping to interpret the action? What gives them authority?

● What additional information are we being given about the participants? Is the information relevant to the sports coverage or concerned with the creation of 'heroes' and 'villains'?

● Replays of key moments: scores, runs, controversies, referees' and umpiring decisions, etc.

Task 4: The studio

How is the studio used to 'frame' and 'anchor' the event to give it a clear sense of narrative progression? How does it link to 'off the pitch' action?

Tips

● Opening
● Advertisements
● Expert commentary
● Trailing the next sequence.

Activity **Analysing sports magazines.**

Task 1

List some basic facts about your magazine, for example:

● how much does it cost?
● how often is it published?

Task 2

Stage 1: What's in a name?
Consider the name of the magazine. What connotations does it have?

Put the name in the middle of an A4 sheet of paper. Spider diagram the connotations.

Stage 2: Front cover
Comment briefly on the central picture:

- who is it?;
- what image is being portrayed?;
- age/gender/ethnicity;
- framing;
- enhancement.

Stage 3: The use of colour
What colours have been selected? Why do you think they have been selected?
Consider:

- logos;
- strips;
- endorsements.

Stage 4: The text
What does the text look like? (Consider typography and layout.)

- Trace the different fonts to isolate the key features and the ways they are reinforced in the text.
- What are the visual patterns?

Stage 5: Stories and features
What types of stories and features are offered? What does this tell you about the target audience?

(Are they interested in: information, gossip, scandal, inside stories, interviews, coaching tips or products and services?)

Stage 6: Evaluation
What is the overall effect of the cover? Who is the magazine aimed at? How do you know?

Task 3
Look through the contents of your magazine:

- What types of articles are there?
- Apart from articles, what else is in the magazine?

Task 4
Study the adverts within the magazine:

- How many are there?
- What types of products are they for?

● How do they reflect the interests/lifestyles of the target audience?

Task 5

Use the Internet to find out more information about the publishers of your magazine:

● are they 'on line'?;
● editorial policy;
● contacting them and other services offered;
● subscription information;
● circulation information;
● the 'values' found on the site in the material presented;
● advertising costs.

Present this information as a poster factfile.

Task 6

Finally, use the information you have researched to produce a short written analysis of your magazine (about 300–500 words). Think particularly about how the magazine promotes sport and what wider representations it offers audiences.

Investigating sport and newspaper language

Extra information

There are three main ways to analyse a news story. (The most detailed analysis will contain elements of all three.)

1. How typical the stories are for the type of paper, i.e. their **genre**.
2. How stories are put together, i.e. their **narrative structure**.
3. How they represent groups, individuals and ideas, i.e. in terms of **representations** and **star status**.

Genre

You can study this in a number of ways:

1. Straightforward content analysis:
    ● number of pages devoted to sport;
    ● types of sport covered;
    ● types of stories;
    ● number and types of photos;
    ● types and styles of headlines.

2. Draw conclusions about:

- most popular sports;
- seriousness of coverage;
- issues of representation (eg where are women's sports? where are the old? where are the paraplegics? etc.).

3. Compare the ways in which a tabloid and a broadsheet have covered the same event. Draw conclusions with regard to:

- style;
- language;
- photos selected; and
- the way in which the event has been treated.

Narrative structure

Stories often revolve around a personal crusade, an element of drama and a hint of aggression. In other words, they may well have a 'hero' who is on a quest and has to overcome an obdurate 'villain' in order to achieve his goal (often, quite literally!). Villains can turn into heroes overnight! Included in the typical narrative pattern are:

- personalisation;
- dramatisation;
- conflict;
- emotional appeal.

Activity **The match report.**

Task

Stage 1
Choose a recent match report.

Stage 2
Comment on the connotations of the headline.

Stage 3
How has the article been 'personalised'?

Stage 4
What is the key confrontation? It is often claimed that sports journalists liken sporting activities to war. Text-mark any evidence of that here.

Stage 5
What narrative does this article have?

Identify the 'hero' and the 'villain'. How did the hero overcome or triumph?

Representations and star status

Activity   The case of David Beckham.

Extra information

What constitutes 'star image' in the world of sport? Based on the work of Dyer, who identified four main components which make up a film star's image, we could say:

1. Their sporting skills: they need to be good at what they do.
2. The non-sporting publicity which surrounds them, for example gossip columns, Hello magazine, etc.
3. News coverage: based on both their sporting skills and their personal life.
4. Criticisms of them: particularly in terms of their sporting performance.

The main differences between a star and a player might be:

- the star's image becomes bigger than their performance;
- their image feeds into different media;
- media coverage ceases to be about their sporting activities: the boundaries between sport and personal life become blurred.

In other words, the cult of a star's personality exists beyond their sport. They become a global phenomenon.

Task

Study the photos of David Beckham below.

Source: © Tony Brady (All Action)   *Source: Stuart Atkins (All Action)*

Stage 1
In what publications would you expect to find these photos? Why?

Stage 2
Suggest captions to anchor each photo.

Stage 3
Compare different groups' responses.

Stage 4
Comment on the image of Beckham that is promoted by each photo.

Stage 5
Imagine that these two photos appeared in the same publication. Draft a headline and outline the report that accompanies it.

INFORMATION FOR TEACHERS

Teaching resources

Exploring Images, McMahon and Quin (Macmillan, 1984) (may be out of print). A good framework for developing skills in responding to images.

Media approaches at Key Stage 4, Barbara H. Connell (**M**edia **E**ducation **W**ales, 1993). Useful units illustrated with pupils' work on advertising, popular television, image and text, Welsh language learners.

Investigating the Welsh Media, Jean Lediard (**MEW**, 1993). Useful units on radio and animation.

Production Practices (English and Media Centre, 1995). Good for a very useful introduction to video work with groups, as well as practical suggestions.

Examining the Media, Connell, Brigley and Edwards (Hodder & Stoughton, 1996). Wide-ranging introduction to GCSE with an emphasis on the WJEC GCSE.

Media Studies for GCSE, Walker and Wall (Collins, 1997). Especially targeted at SEG GCSE.

GCSE Media Studies, Bowker (Hodder & Stoughton, 1998). Especially targeted at OCEA GCSE.

Media. New Ways and Meanings, Stuart and Kowaltzke (2nd ed., Jacaranda (Australia), 1997).

Film Language. A Study Guide (+ video) (Film Education). Expensive but very useful on film language.

The Advertising Pack and *The Soap Pack* (English and Media Centre). Both are invaluable in their areas.

GSCE Resources (Relay Publications, 1998), available from **M**edia **E**ducation **W**ales:

- *Pop Music*, Debbie Jones. Introduces the concept of genre through lots of small activities.
- *Television Sport*, Steve Jenkins. Concentrates on the World Cup coverage but lots of insights into production practices.

- *Animating Women*, Sarah Evans. Difficult but some of the activities could certainly be modified at this level.
- *Reading Images*, Gill Eames-Jones. A basic introduction to working with still images. Very approachable.
- *Television Drama*, Moira Strevens. Well-organised approach to covering the basic starting points.
- *Animation*, John Ashton. Excellent introduction to a fascinating area. Good practical tips and ideas.

Top of the Pops Mix Factory CD-ROM (BBC). Making music tracks, pop videos, playlists, links to 'Top of the Pops' website: good fun.

Backtracks CD-ROM (Channel 4). Excellent projects using video clips, music and sound effects.

INFORMATION FOR GCSE CANDIDATES

General

- All the examination boards who offer Media Studies split the assessment between coursework and a written examination.
- Coursework counts for 50 per cent.
- The written examination counts for 50 per cent.
- These are added together for the final grade.
- All boards tier the written paper.
- No boards tier the coursework.
- Foundation Tier: candidates are awarded G–C grades.
- Higher Tier: candidates are awarded E–A* grades.
- Candidates can be ungraded on both tiers.

Tip

Be guided by your teacher as to the best way to achieve high grades in Media Studies.

Coursework

Extra information

The requirements for the three examination groups vary. However, they each have two common components: production work and assignments.

Production work

Overview of production process and evaluation

Look at Figure IC.1

Extra information

- Every stage of the production process will be evaluated. This can be done in a variety of ways: discussion, drafting versions of layouts, improvising ('hot seating'), rehearsing, 'brainstorming', text-marking, spider diagramming.
- Keep records.
- You improve your grades by reflecting critically on what you have achieved.

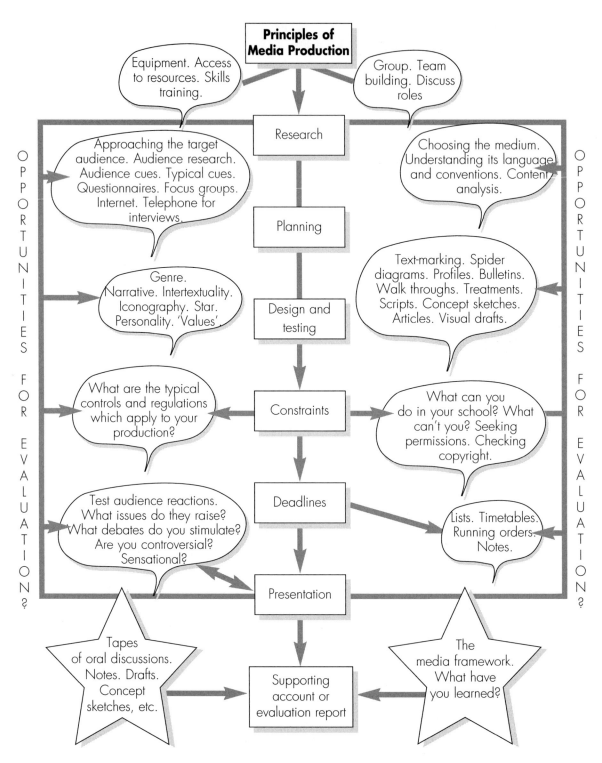

Figure IC.1

Tip

'Critically' means showing:

- what you know of the key ideas which influence media production
- your knowledge and understanding of the form and genre of your media production
- typical conventions you have explored from a personal viewpoint.

Producing reports and accounts

- Present your material in appropriate media forms.
- If written, make a **title page**, use **headings**, **visual information**, consider the needs of your **audience**, **construct in clear stages** and come to a clear **concluding section**.
- If in other forms: audio/video report/HTML, then the conventions of those **'languages'** should apply.
- In short, as all good media students do, construct a narrative with clear stages!

Activity   **Assignments**

Extra information

- The Activities in this book are assignments of a very great variety.
- You need, with the assistance of your teacher, to choose your best assignments to present for coursework.
- You teacher will advise you of the requirements of your syllabus.

10 top tips

1. Keep to deadlines. Work does not go away.
2. Get into the habit of jotting things down or recording your thoughts and ideas on a portable tape recorder as you go through the various activities.
3. Check what the media are up to (especially in the area which you are studying).
4. Be helpful and co-operative in group work, but make sure your views are considered.
5. Take control of your own learning. The media are so diverse that you will always find aspects worth studying more deeply. Use your own resources – family, friends and people you know – they all have views on the media and long media histories which you can draw on.
6. Be bold and inventive like some of the media students featured in

this book. Do not just copy things that already exist. Put a personal stamp on existing forms.

7. Present all your work carefully. Presentation is a key media skill.

8. Use your own interests, enthusiasms and experience as starting points for exploration. You may be a performer (sport, pop, drama), fan (contributor to chat rooms, memorabilia collector, film or video collector), compulsive drawer (comic characters, animation), web page designer. When you grow up(!) you might want to be a fashion model or a football commentator. Use the media framework to develop these interests.

9. Respond positively to questions about your work. Listen. Take on board. Question and defend sometimes.

10. Learn the 'languages of the media' by asking questions yourself.

The written paper

Information

OCR

A written paper based on:

- description and analysis of unseen video and print extracts;
- questions on selected topic areas.

SEG

A controlled test on a specified topic area.

WJEC

A written paper based on:

- stimulus material from video/radio (specified areas) and print-based materials (comics, newspapers and magazines).

INDEX

Page numbers in **bold type** refer to definitions.

advertising
  films 142–3, 144–5
  magazines covers 41
  posters 13–14, 17, 142–3
  on radio 170–72
  sport 189
albums **154**
analogue television 92
anchors 4, 7, 161
animation 71, 173, 188
audience signs
  colour 37–8
  language 38
  position 37
  treatment 37
audiences
  active 42
  expectations 99, 109–10
  foreknowledge **138**
  fragmented 100
  identification 31
  targeting 33–4, 34
  television ratings 96–7

Beatles 149
Beckham, David 197
body language 3, 9
branding 92, 162
broadcast networks 95
Broadcasters' Audience Research Board [BARB]
  96–7
Brookside 107–8

camera lenses 3, 135

camerawork
  angles 3, 8, 136
  illusions 136
  shot sizes 3, 130
  shot types 105, 126, 130
  space 135–6
captions 4, 7, 38
cartoons
  film characters 23
  frames **24**
  importance 18
  links **24**
  narratives 22, 23
  panels **24**
  points of view **24**
  shots **24**
  stereotypes 29, 31
  universal language 28–9, 30
catagorisation 31
CD covers 153
characters 6, 7, 9
  films 126, 140, 141
  identification with 128
  police series 110
  Propp's theory 127
  star's image 141
  television 105–6
chart music 146–7
chat shows
  audiences 117
  complaints 121
  controversial 117
  dumbing down 116
  fake guests 118–21

chat shows – *cont.*
  format 116
  presenters 116, 117
clothes 9
colour, use of 3, 37–8
comedy
  expectation 166
  logical sequences 166
  narrative 166
  punchlines 166
  radio 165–7
  stereotypes 166
commentators 193
compilations 156
complaints, chat shows 121
composition 3
computer games
  addiction 184
  animation 173, 186
  arcade **174**
  benefits 177
  combat **174**
  consumers 179–82
  criticisms 177, 184
  female representation 173, 175–7, 186–8
  industry 173, 174
  narrative structures 174–5
  racing **174**
  reviews 173
  role play **174**
  simulations **174**
  stars 185–6
  stereotypes 175
connotation 6, 7
consumers, computer games 179–82
critical analysis 32
Croft, Lara 186–7
cropping, photographs 3–4
cross-overs, media 78, 163
current affairs, reporters 78

dead time 133
deconstruction 7, 22

denotation 6, 7
digital television 92
directors 128
Disney organisation 68, 70
documentaries 53–4
  points of view 151
  pop music 151
  producers 57–8, 60–61
drama
  adaptations 167
  faction 167
  issues 107–8
  narrators 167
  radio 167–8
  reconstructions 167
  soaps 93, 102, 167
  television 93, 94, 105–6
drawings, manipulation 44–5
dress codes 3
dumbing down 79, 116

EastEnders 102
editing
  news programmes 79
  time alteration 133–4
  videos 60, 62–3
electronic newspapers 789
establishment shots 126
eye movements 3
eyeline matching 126

faction 167
fake guests, chat shows 118–21
fanzines **152**
female representation 45–6, 173, 175–7, 186–8
films
  adaptations 138
  advertising 142–3, 144–5
  characters 126, 128, 140, 141
  directors 128
  distribution 125
  films of 144

generic codes 124
Hollywood system 125, 140
lighting 135, 136
original 138
posters 142–3
prequels 138, **139**
shooting 126, 135–6
silent 139
stars 139–40, 141, 142
structures 125
television series 138
time alterations 133–4
trailers 142, 143–4
film noir 128, **129**
foreknowledge **138**
formats
adventures 100
series 94
television 94, 99–100
frames **2**
breaking 2
cartoons **24**
constructing 24, 131
filming 135
links **24**
rules 131
single 24
freebies **150**

gender
computer games 173, 175–7, 186–8
representation 45–6, 173, 175–7, 186–8
role-reversal 127
genres 31, 43, 77
buddy films 101–2
chat shows 116–18
documentaries 54
films 124, 141, 142
pop music 146–7
radio 163
stars 142
teams 102
global conglomerates 68

Hollywood Studio system 125, 140
humour
bitter 21
messages 18
puns 21
recognition 18
visual 18, 21
wacky [zany] 21

images
altered 3–4
captions 4
constructing 9
deconstruction 7
manipulating 4
'imagineering' 68
Internet
marketing films 145
minority interests 162
pop music 147
radio 162
sport 189
intertextuality 36–7, **36**
interviews 151
computer games 179–82
documentary producer 57–8, 60–61

lighting codes 3, 8
linguistic signs 38
locations 7, 9
lyrics 146, **147**

magazines
audience signs 37–8
covers 41
documentary 53–4
fanzines **152**
linking 33
photostories 49–50
point of sale 32
pop music 159
sports 152, 189, 193–5
stereotypes 36

magazines – *cont.*
  targeting 32–3, 34, 159
Manic Street Preachers 153–5
marketing
  chat shows 144
  film prizes 145
  films of films 144
  free publicity 144
  freebies **150**
  Internet 145
  interviews 145
  music links 144
  pop music 147
  reviews 145
  spin-offs 68, 75, 144–5
media
  competition 96
  industries **91**
  industry 190
  'language' 91
  organisation values 78
  technology 91
memorabilia **147**
mise-en-scéne **2–3**, 23, 136
montage **3**
Murdoch, Rupert 189–90
music *see* pop music

narrative structures
  animation 71–2
  cartoons 22, 23
  comedy 166
  computer games 174–5
  documentaries 54
  films 127
  police series 110–12
  sports reporting 196
narratives 8, 9
  omniscient 128, **129**
  restricted 128, **129**
  theories 127
  voice quality 60
narrators 167

narrowcasting 95, 162, 171
news
  agencies 83
  initiatives 79
  reporters 78, 86
  sensationalising 79
  truth 78
news programmes
  dumbing down 79
  editing 79
  production 79
  radio 84, 86
  running orders 87
  television 88–9, 90, 94
newscasters 78
newspapers
  electronic 789
  sport 195–6
  targeting 80
niche programming 95
non-verbal communication 3, 9

omniscient narrative 128, **129**

photographs, cropping 3–4
photostories 49–50
pitches 105
planetonsunday 81–3
planetsport 85
plots 22
point of sale 32
points of view [PoV] 7, 8, 9
  cartoons **24**
  documentaries 53, 151
  news 78
police series
  characters 110
  expectations 109–10
  narrative 110–12
  scheduling 109
pop music
  CD covers 153
  albums **154**

compilations 156
credits **154**
documentaries 151
fan identity 147
genres 146–7
industry 146
Internet 147
magazines 159
marketing 147
promoters 146
radio 147
television 150
videos 156–7
posters **13**
conventions 14–15
films 142–3
location 13, 17
purposes 13–14
prequels 138, **139**
presenters
chat shows 116, 117
talkback shows 164–5
privacy, stars 103, 197
production
news programmes 79
police series 112
process 201–3
Propp, Vladimir 127
props 3, 9
punchlines 166
puns 21

radio
advertising on 170–72
anchors 161
branding 162
characteristics 161
comedy 165–7
commercial 170–71
drama 167–8
Internet 162
local/regional 162, 171
minority interests 162

narrowcasting 95, 162
news 84, 86
pop music 147
sport 189, 191–3
talkback 164
television transfers 163
ratings, television 96–7
real time 133
recognition signs 34
record promoters 146
regulations, television 108
reporters 78, 84, 86
representations 6
restricted narrative 128, **129**
rockumentaries 151, **151**

scheduling, television 98–9
settings 3, 9
'short cuts' 31
shots
cartoons **24**
characters 126
close up 130, 136
distance 135–6
establishment 126
eyeline matching 126
fade-outs 126
interaction 126
long 130
medium 130
rules 131
simultaneous 126
sizes 3, 130
sitcoms 165
soaps
radio 167
television 93
sound bites **152**
spin-offs 68, 75
sponsorship, sport 189
sport
advertising 189
commentaries 193

sport – *cont.*
  Internet 189
  magazines 152, 189, 193–5
  minority 190
  monopolies 191
  nationalism 190–91
  newspapers 195–6
  radio 189, 191–3
  sponsorship 189
  stars 197
  television 3, 189, 191–3
stars
  computer games 185–6
  exploitation 102–3
  films 139–40, 141, 142
  Hollywood system 125, 140
  names 140
  news items 103
  privacy 103, 197
  publicity 102
  sport 197
  television 102
stereotypes
  cartoons 29, 31
  comedy 166
  computer games 175
  magazines 36
story construction 8
storyboards 115
sub-editors 79

talkback shows 164–5
target audiences 32–3, 34, 80
  narrowcasting 95, 162, 171
television
  analogue 92
  audience sizes 96–7
  characters 105–6
  chat shows 116–23
  competition 96
  digital 92

drama 93, 94, 105–6
formats 94
narrowcasting 95
news 88–9, 90, 94
niche programming 95
police series 109–13
pop music 150
popular 96
radio transfers 163
regulations 108
scheduling 98–9
series 94
soaps 93, 102
sport 3, 189, 191–3
stars 102
time slots 97–8
trailers 99
viewers 93
time
  accelerated 133–4
  dead 133
  real 133
  reversed 134
  slowing 134
  stopped 134
time slots 97–8
Torodov, Tzvetan 127
Toy Story, spin-offs 75
trailers
  films 142, 143–4
  television 99

Under*currents* 57–8, 60–61

videos
  campaigning 58, 59, 60–61
  editing 60, 62–3
  pop music 156–7
voice overs 60, 61, 128

Who Wants to be a Millionaire 95